Jardine's Last Tour

India 1933–34

First published in Great Britain by Methuen 2011

Copyright © Tim Heald 2011

Methuen
8 Artillery Row
London
SW1P 1RZ

1 3 5 7 9 10 8 6 4 2

www.methuen.co.uk

ISBN 978-0-413-77697-6

Set in Garamond by SX Composing DTP, Rayleigh, Essex

Printed and bound by CPI Group (UK) Ltd, Croydon, CR0 4YY

A CIP catalogue record for this book is available from the British Library

Jardine's Last Tour

India 1933–34

Tim Heald

Methuen

Contents

List of Illustrations		vii
Dedication		ix
Introduction		1
Chapter 1	Indian Cricket in the 1930s	4
Chapter 2	The Touring Party	12
Chapter 3	Home from Home	26
Chapter 4	Opening Salvos	33
Chapter 5	Cricketing Grandees	40
Chapter 6	Big Game	52
Chapter 7	First Test Match, Bombay	72
Chapter 8	Second Test Match, Calcutta	79
Chapter 9	First Defeat	92
Chapter 10	Third Test Match, Madras	107
Chapter 11	Aftermath	118
Appendices		121
Select Bibliography		137
Index		138

List of Illustrations

All reproduced by kind permission of the Roger Mann Collection

The MCC touring party on board RMS *Moolton* en route to India

MCC begin their first innings against NW Frontier Province at Peshawar on the first turf pitch of the tour

MCC and the Punjab Governor's XI before the match at Lahore

C F Walters and the Maharaja of Patiala toss up before the match between MCC and Northern India at Lahore

The MCC tourists are welcomed at the Parsee Gymkhana in Bombay

The second Test at Calcutta. Sleeping guards protecting the pitch

The two captains, Douglas Jardine and Major C K Nayudu, before the second Test match at Calcutta

An invitation to dinner for C F Walters from the Viceroy on the first evening of the second Test match at Calcutta

MCC versus Maharaja Kumar of Vizianagram's XI at Benares. Vizzy's XI are in the field. His palace is in the background

MCC versus Maharaja Kumar of Vizianagram's XI at Benares. Vizzy batting in front of his palace

C F Walters leads out the MCC against Central India at Indore. Daly's College is in the background

The three Nayudu brothers, from left – Major C K, C S, C L

Both teams before the match between MCC and the Nawab of Moin-ud-Dowlah's XI at Secunderabad

The four page engagement schedule for the Governor of Madras MCC leaving from Central Station, Bombay

Percy Fender wishes Douglas Jardine 'bon voyage' as he sets out for
the Indian tour of 1933-34.

Douglas Jardine queueing outside the Oval
on the first day of the final Test between
England and Australia, August 1934.

Dedication

For Mansur Ali Khan, known to us as the Nawab of Pataudi or Tiger who demonstrated to me that cricket could be sweaty, poetic and sometimes even majestic.

Introduction

Douglas Jardine was one of the most controversial cricketers of his day. His exploits as England captain on the Ashes tour in 1932-33, during the acrimonious 'Bodyline' series, brought him a notoriety which remained for the rest of his life. We, that is England, won the Ashes but we did not make friends and the Australians did not think we were playing cricket. Jardine believed that the game was there to be won and by deploying his fast bowlers, very fast, in an intimidating yet lawful, way he and we won. The Australians complained at the highest possible level and it is only now that this whingeing is being questioned.

On his return from the tour of Australia, Jardine received a welcome which took him by surprise. He was met at Euston station by a number of MCC officials including Lord Hawke, Lord Lewisham and Sir Kynaston Studd and given the club's ambivalence while he was down under, this was itself an occasion of surprise. Another surprise came when MCC asked him to captain the England team against the West Indies, who would be on tour in 1933 and would play three Test matches. Jardine accepted the appointment for to have declined would have appeared churlish. MCC were still showing strong support for their captain despite some misgivings.

The 1933 season was a quiet one for Jardine. He played in just seven matches for his county, Surrey, and four other first class fixtures. Against the West Indies, he played in the first two Test matches at Lord's and Old Trafford but missed the third Test due to injury. In the Old Trafford match, Jardine scored his maiden Test century. The West Indian pace bowlers used bodyline tactics against England's batsmen, particularly Jardine, and bowled intimidatingly fast and not always at the stumps. Faced with criticism from press and public, MCC, as custodians of the laws of cricket, concluded that changes would be necessary.

The MCC/England party for India was announced in August 1933 and immediately caused some disquiet with the hosts. It included just two members of the successful Ashes party, the captain and Verity the Yorkshire spinner, and some in India took this as an insult. However the 'second division' England players would prove much too strong for their Indian opposition.

Jardine's appointment as captain was not made lightly as the minutes of the MCC Committee meeting for 10 July 1933 show. 'After a prolonged discussion it was decided to invite Mr D. R. Jardine to captain the team and to ask the President and Treasurer [Lords Hailsham and Hawke] of the MCC to have a talk with him when the official invitation was extended.'

This 'talk' was presumably to remind Jardine of the consequences of antagonising Indian crowds and Indian cricket officialdom. Jardine was happy to be returning to India, the country of his birth, but any emotions he might have experienced were soon forgotten, as beating the opposition became paramount.

The Indian tour proved to be Jardine's 'swan-song'. On his return to England in 1934, he announced that he would not be available for the series against Australia, a decision no doubt welcomed by MCC, or for his county, Surrey. He joined the *Evening Standard* and reported on the Test series which saw Australia regain the Ashes with two wins in the five matches. Bradman whom Jardine had set out to contain in the 1932-33 series, (though he averaged 56.57), scored 758 runs for an average of 94.75.

So Jardine's cricket career ended on an unsatisfactory note. He had played in 22 Tests and as captain in 15 of them. His record as captain was nine victories, five drawn games and one loss. But his Test career was too short and too controversial for the accolade of 'great captain' to be bestowed on him. Had he played in the 1934 series against Australia and retained the 'Ashes', few contemporary commentators would have doubted his right to a place among the 'greats'. However it was not to be. In the winter of 1934-35, MCC were determined to eradicate 'bodyline' and made changes to the laws which achieved it. Jardine was pretty much *persona non grata*. There exists a rather poignant photograph of him queuing with members of the public to gain entry to the Oval on the first day of the last Test match of the 1934 series. What a difference a year had made.

In 1934 Jardine married Irene Margaret, the grand-daughter of William Barclay Peat, founder of the accountancy firm W B Peat & Co, later Peat, Marwick, Mitchell, now KPMG. He had to support his wife and later, four children but his business career was only moderately successful and the family was often struggling. Douglas Jardine died in 1958. He was only 57 years old.

I have long been fascinated by him and by his place in the history of the game. Like a later England captain, Mike Brearley, he was a fine leader who was able to get the best out of Larwood just as Brearley was able to coax superlatives from Ian Botham. He was an unusual man and he would probably have been more at home in later less stuffy times. Great cricketer maybe not; great captain, I think the case is unanswerable.

The early 1930s were also an unusual time in the evolution of Indian cricket and of the sub-continent in more general terms. I wanted to write about Jardine's last tour, about the end of one kind of India and the birth of another. I felt this would be worth recording in a book albeit not in a long one. The result is a shortish one of around 30,000 words. It gave me an opportunity to research in the library at MCC and also in the dying months of the National Newspaper Library in Colindale, North London. For both I am profoundly grateful and I am also grateful to Jardine and his team who travelled around the Raj playing cricket, shooting game, behaving raffishly at times and providing all of us with a fascinating historical footnote of some significance in the history of the British Empire.

There are still people who believe that cricket is just a game and that Douglas Jardine was only a player. Neither belief is true.

Tim Heald
Martock
July 2011

1

Indian Cricket in the 1930s

The top honour in the Indian New Year's Honours list of 1933 went to the whiskery, belligerent looking Maharaja of Kashmir who was awarded the Grand Cross of the Order of the Star of India. It was proof, if any were needed that the aristocracy in the sub-continental Raj were still ubiquitous and seemingly all-powerful, not least in the world of cricket. When the Cricket Club of India was founded along similar lines to MCC, on the last day of the England versus Australia Test match in Brisbane, that year, the Patron was the Maharaja of Porbandar.

Another Indian aristocrat, the Nawab of Pataudi, was in Douglas Jardine's MCC team that toured Australia in 1932/33 and scored a century in the first Test at Sydney. He also played in the second Test at Melbourne but was dropped for the third in favour of the dour Lancastrian professional Eddie Paynter, a decision that caused almost as much outrage in India as the "bodyline" bowling devised by Jardine and executed by Harold Larwood. Pataudi, a wristy batsman and old-fashioned Corinthian disagreed with his captain over such tactics and this was apparently why he was dropped. He did not feature in the rest of the series though he played later against New South Wales wearing a panama hat which kept blowing off in the wind, to the delight and amusement of the crowd.

In England, always described as "home" in the *Times of India*, another gentlemanly Indian cricketer, K.S. Duleepsinhji, nephew of the famous Jam Sahib of Nawanagar, supported Jardine's bowling tactics and said that if the Australians couldn't stand up to Larwood they should play with a soft tennis ball. (A.W. Carr, Larwood's peppery captain at Nottingham suggested that if the Australians couldn't cope with the fast bowler they should make him bowl "underhand".)

Had he not been unwell "Duleep" would almost certainly have gone to Australia with MCC. Despite his education at Cheltenham and Cambridge he had been mooted as the first Indian captain of the national team but he rejected the country of his birth and instead chose to lead Sussex like his uncle Ranjitsinhji before him.

Men such as Ranji, known to many British who had trouble pronouncing his name as "Rum Ginger Whisky", were fabulously rich and, though they often improved the lot of their subjects with inspired schemes for the infrastructure of their bailiwicks they also cultivated an absurd, not to say decadent life-style in emulation of the most extravagant excesses of the West.

Ranji, for instance, had a close relationship with the French jeweller Jacques Cartier. He featured in the amazing 2009 exhibition, *Maharaja* at London's Victoria and Albert Museum. In the book which accompanied the exhibition, Amin Jaffer, the head of Asian Art at Christie's who helped curate the exhibition, wrote that Ranji was a "skilled designer himself . . . His design for a sliding cigarette case was taken up by Asprey's and put into production." Ranji used to travel about with suitcases full of items from his State collection as well as rings, watches and ornaments. He acquired the fabulous 136.25 carat Queen of Holland diamond which was renamed the Ranjitsinhji and became the centrepiece of a multi-stranded necklace designed by Cartier himself.

There was considerable rivalry among these cricketing princes. Some such as Ranji, Duleep and Pataudi were brilliant players. Others such as Porbandar and the portly, portentous Vizzy, Kumar of Vizianagram, were relative duffers. The Maharaja of Patiala came somewhere in between but suffered from having fallen out with the Viceroy, the Earl of Willingdon, who in the days of his untitled youth, when he was plain Mr. Freeman Freeman-Thomas, had been good enough to win a cricket blue at Cambridge.

Patiala, a compulsive womaniser with a large number of concubines in his service was said to have made an unwelcome pass at one of Willingdon's daughters at a ball in Simla. There were strong rumours that Patiala was drunk at the time. At the annual Delhi cricket festival in February it was announced that "contrary to expectations the Maharaja of Patiala could not come". The Maharaja of Porbandar took his place and the faintly ludicrous Kumar of Vizianagram also took part. The real reason for these substitutions was not made public but privately gossip was rife.

The Maharaja of Patiala was almost impossibly grand. He was reputed to have fathered 88 children by his ten marriages and his numerous concubines. He favoured a motorised cavalcade of twenty Rolls Royce limousines and he had erected a unique transport system in his home town known as the Patiala State Monorail Tramway. At the time of the match in Patiala against Jardine's tourists he had just celebrated his forty-second birthday.

His full title was Lieutenant-General His Highness Farzand-i-Khas-i-Dhaulat-i-Inglishia, Mansur-i-Zaman, Amir ul-Umara, Maharajaddhiraja Raj Rajeshwar, 108 Sri Maharaja-i-Rajgan, Maharaja Sir Bhupinder Singh, Mahendra Bahadur, Yadu Vansha Vatans Bhatti Kul Bushan, Maharaja of Patiala, GCSI, GCIE, GCVO, GBE. In his photograph, moustached, turbaned, exquisitely jewelled, and wearing some of the medals from a collection which was rumoured to be the largest in the world, he stares out haughtily from below lowered lids. He died a few years later aged only forty-six but in 1933 he was Chancellor of the Indian Chamber of Princes and had represented India at the League of Nations in 1925. He was one of the grandest rulers in the world and he obviously knew it. The Maharaja was not a man to be trifled with.

Like Ranji, he was keen on jewellery. When he visited Paris in 1928 he brought along six iron chests full of jewels which he presented to Louis Boucheron. Boucheron turned the 7,000 diamonds, 14,000 emeralds and numerous sapphires, rubies and pearls into 149 individual pieces. Shortly afterwards Cartier exhibited an earlier collection of commissions, also from Patiala. These included two fabulous diamond necklaces which also featured in the V and A exhibition of 2009 and were part of what remains "the largest single commission that Cartier has ever executed".

The Viceroy hated Patiala. It wasn't just the wealth and power which threatened Lord Willingdon but the story of the vice-regal ball in Simla concerning His Lordship's unmarried daughter. His Lordship was not amused.

After the well-contested match and much lavish hospitality Jardine suggested that his host might like to turn out for his team in the match against the Viceroy's team in Delhi a few days later. After all Patiala was a member of the MCC and had indeed played a number of matches for them in 1926 and 1927. The suggestion infuriated the Viceroy. Jardine informed him as a courtesy but Willingdon was livid and ordered Jardine to withdraw the invitation immediately. The MCC captain did as he was told but he was not pleased. He took his revenge on the field of play and inflicted a comprehensive defeat on the Viceroy's team. Willingdon had previously been Governor-General of Canada and gives the impression of having been a fairly disagreeable person.

Cricket is and was important in India. The historian Ramachandra Guha has written an entire volume about the game there, subtitled *The Indian History of a British Sport*. Maria Misra, the Oxford academic, a Fellow of Keble College, includes material on the game in her general history of *India since the Great Rebellion*. Misra implies that "The British saw India as a set of competing cricket teams to be marshalled into sportsmanly co-existence under the tutelage of an all-powerful umpire." Guha believes that "cricket has always been a microcosm of the fissures and tensions within Indian Society".

Certainly cricket mattered in a way that is not accepted by many academic historians. For the British, epitomised by Lord Willingdon, it was a symbol of British rule and a means of government. In this view Willingdon was supported by such men as Lord Harris, the great cricket guru and for a time Governor of Bombay, and of Jardine himself. For others, including the left-wing academic

Guha and Maria Misra, cricket also had a more nationalist even democratic dimension. On the one hand anglophile princes such as Ranji and Duleep; on the other the "Untouchable" low-caste spin bowler Palwankar Baloo, considered by Guha to be "the first great Indian cricketer".

Cricket in the sub-continent could be considered in a number of different ways but, as the very existence of serious historians such as Guha and Misra suggests, it was important. Elsewhere it might be thought of as just a game but not in the Raj. It was a metaphor and a symbol but it was also a reality. Indian cricket was central to the evolution of India.

A formal invitation to "The M.C.C." was issued by Antony de Mello, the Secretary of the Indian Board of Cricket. De Mello asked the club to tour in 1933 and 1934 and it was hoped that India would be allotted three Test matches. This proved to be the case but to widespread dismay these three matches were scheduled for Bombay, New Delhi and Secunderabad. Calcutta was fobbed off with a match between the touring team and an Army XI. Bengal was so furious that its cricket association threatened to break off relations with the rest of the country. As a result the schedule was amended so that Delhi and Secunderabad were dropped and Calcutta and Madras took their places. This prompted fury from Secunderabad, which was in effect a joint city with Hyderabad and had, according to one angry local cricket supporter, been "for several years a prominent theatre of first-class cricket". The anonymous writer continued "It goes without saying that Calcutta, though it may claim to be 'the second city of the Empire' is a nonentity in cricket."

The final itinerary began with a match in Karachi which was then part of a united India, the independent nation of Pakistan was still some 14 years into the future. After Karachi the tourists were then expected to fulfil a leisurely programme around the sub-continent.

If cricket was unrecognisable then British India was even more so. Underneath the thin red line the sub-continent carried on in the essentially unchanging, unchanged fashion of many hundreds of years. On to this unwavering historical pattern was grafted a tier populated by alien rulers and their acolytes. England, or more accurately, Britain was home. The ships of the Orient line – the *Orama*, the *Oransay*, the *Otranto* and the *Orantes* had "homeward" sailings culminating in Plymouth and London. The fast oil-burning twin-screw mail boats of the Bibby Line also went "home". At the Roxy "a cool, clean and comfortable talkie theatre" in down-town Bombay, *Jack's the Boy* starred Jack Hulbert and Cicely Courtneidge and was described as "the greatest comedy ever seen".

The Taj Mahal hotel staged a cocktail dance between 7.00 and 8.30 at which an Italian orchestra provided music for such new-fangled dances as the Rumba, the Ranchero, the Paso Doble and the Tango. Durable dusters could be purchased for three shillings and eight pence a dozen. Butter and cream, suitably graded, came in tins. *Red Ensign* coffee was India's best "picked and prepared from the choicest Beans grown on the high altitudes of the Nilgiri Hills of Southern India". Internal travel was by trains with names like the *Madras Mail*, the *Deccan Queen* and the *Allahabad Express*. You could buy folding tortoise shell spectacles and Cawtex Ladies Tennis Socks. "After a strenuous game a refreshing bath with Scrubbs' cloudy ammonia allays irritation from mosquito bites." The *Illustrated Weekly of India* was serialising "The Mask of Fu Manchu" by Sax Rohmer and described it as "The tale of a sinister, inscrutable Chinaman who menaced the whole Western world with destruction". As far as the magazine was concerned the Raj put India firmly in the Eastern camp. Not everyone would agree.

In many important respects India was just like home, home being a sort of antimacassered dream set in Cheltenham, Tunbridge Wells or Eastbourne. Every so often chaps and their wives went to those and other places on restorative leave. Even accounts of the cricket matches played around the Raj were peppered with such phrases as "stepped into the breach" and "checked the rot". Everything was a peculiar mixture of gentility and ruthlessness, rough often racist justice and perfect manners. It was hot, of course, devilishly so and every summer the Viceroy's court decamped to the hills of Simla where it was cooler and the conifers reminded everyone of Bournemouth. The place was also full of Indians which was, perhaps, unfortunate. However they made excellent servants and the best were wonderfully loyal.

Sometimes the attempt to graft safe, dependable, conservative "home" on to the exoticism and spice of the sub-continent led to chaos, confusion, misconception and absurdity. A review of an S.P.B. Mais book called *The Unknown Island* conceded that the expatriate's view of England was often wrong and out-of-date. The real England, as portrayed by someone such as Mais who actually lived there, was often elusive. The true Mais version sometimes "astonishes those of us whose vista of England during the short months of leave is mainly a desolate expanse of tarmacadam, petrol pumps and hoardings".

The divergent cultures produced a collision as often as a marriage. One day, for example, "The Bombay Hunt" enjoyed "a very good day's sport". On another a cricket match produced a sensation when, in the staid language of the *Times of India*, "The Railway captain announced the withdrawal of the team, alleging that the umpire's decisions were unfavourable. The spectators, not apparently appreciating their attitude requested them to continue but in vain". A Jain girl wanted to become a nun and "a large female panther was recently killed at Bhanoji, a village in the Koloba District by Mrs. Southerland, a well-known shikari of Khandala." In another part of the country an Englishman was killed by a wild buffalo, enraged by being wounded by his first, non-lethal shot. A money-lender was allegedly killed by two Brahmins in a "gruesome murder".

Life in the Indian Raj was dangerous in a timeless way. A wife was sold for a hundred rupees; a reward was offered for the killing of a man-eating tiger; a European was stabbed; the *Punjab Mail* was derailed by terrorists while in Jubbulpore a cyclone derailed more railway wagons; a terrorist den was raided in Madras; in Bombay there was a serious fight between Hindu and Christian milkmen; in Mysore lightning caused havoc.

Even for the cosseted ruling class, with their reassuring reminders of home, with its safety and order, life could be primitive and threatening. In Lower Bengal some explorers were chased by alligators and in the Central Provinces an Army officer, a colonel no less, was stung to death by killer bees while innocently exploring a cave. In Burma an officer was shot dead by his butler.

This was also the era of Mahatma Gandhi. He was the uncomfortable, unprecedented focus for Indian nationalism and for the voice of independence. The British found him difficult to deal with because his methods were essentially non-violent and he was rational, democratic and very difficult to dismiss as a dangerous, violent revolutionary. At the time of the Jardine tour the Mahatma was pursuing different objectives, campaigning not against the foreign tyranny of British rule but at the home-grown inequalities of the caste system. "Mr. Gandhi to fast again" ran one headline, explaining that this 21 day fast was "unconditional and irrevocable" and was "against no-one in particular but in the interests of 'greater purity'". Not all his followers were happy. The Untouchables whose cause he espoused were dismayed. "Your decision is fatal to our cause", they protested. "We want you to live. Pray do not fast." Fast, however, he did, though not before consuming a final meal of six Jaffa oranges.

2

The Touring Party

Douglas Jardine was in many ways the most obvious candidate to captain the MCC's cricket team in India in 1933–34. For a start, he was the incumbent, and although the tour of Australia which has subsequently become notorious for its hostile 'bodyline' bowling, Jardine and his men had won. Moreover the authorities had – sort of and up to a point - stuck by their man as, for the most part, had his team. MCC had been rattled by Australian reactions to Jardine's tactics and by the Australian Board's hostile telegrams; but they had held their nerve. Some of his players such as the Nawab of Pataudi made their displeasure clear and others such as, apparently, Voce and Allen preferred not to travel under him again; but, on the whole, the players were loyal.

Christopher Martin-Jenkins, best of the post-Swanton generation of cricket journalists, and currently President of MCC, described Jardine as "inflexibly determined" and he gave the impression of being both rigorous and ruthless. These were, oddly enough, much the same characteristics as those venerated by many Australians when deployed on their own side and exemplified by the greatest of all Australian cricketers, Sir Donald Bradman.

Bradman's tactics when using his own very fast and dangerous bowlers, Lindwall and Miller, were not unlike Jardine's when he was ordering Larwood to bowl "leg theory". I well remember Denis Compton telling me ruefully that after Lindwall, bowling in tandem with Miller, felled him at Old Trafford, he tried to "knock my block off" all over again. I'm not convinced that Australia in the 1930s had a batsman as courageous – or unconventionally touched by genius – as Compton. Nor did they have any bowlers much faster than Alec Bedser who was the swiftest man in England's attack in 1948.

In the aftermath of the controversial tour Jardine was rejected by the establishment and most significantly by the Marylebone Cricket Club. His players, notably Larwood himself, remained loyal, often beyond duty. At a private dinner the team presented their captain with a silver cigar box and Herbert Sutcliffe, a dour Yorkshire professional to his boot laces, praised Jardine in heartfelt words. "I cannot tell you how much we all appreciated playing under you", he said, "how much we admired your skill, courage, fighting spirit and the way in which you upheld the best traditions of English cricket. Our games in Australia were by no means as pleasant as they might have been. Nevertheless we had the satisfaction of knowing that we were playing under a great skipper, a great fighter and a man under whom we all felt privileged to serve. Every cricketer owed you a debt of gratitude for the glorious fight you made, which placed England at the head of international cricket."

Most Australians hated Jardine and he was by some way the most unpopular Pom captain to tour down under. His boss, the joint manager P.F. "Plum" later Sir Pelham Warner also won the Ashes as a captain in Australia in 1903/04, but was perceived as an altogether more benign and genial figure. That may be the case but Warner and Jardine came from remarkably similar backgrounds. Warner's family had made a somewhat disreputable fortune in Trinidad whereas Jardine's father and grandfather were both eminent lawyers in the Raj – his grandfather rose to be Lord Chief Justice. Warner was educated at Rugby and Oriel College, Oxford; Jardine at Winchester and New College, Oxford. Both captained the university and Warner was just as addicted to the "Harlequin" quartered cap which attracted such Antipodean antipathy when sported by Jardine. Warner who was awarded it when representing Oxford against Yorkshire once said that he would no sooner go into bat without it than "jump over the moon". Jardine evidently felt the same and, like Warner, preferred to wear it rather than the cap of his county or country. In Warner's case it was regarded as a harmless eccentricity.

When Jardine wore it in Australia it was as a red rag to the proverbial bull.

Nevertheless Jardine was not as patrician a figure as he appeared to Australians and to subsequent history. Indeed he is, in many ways as much a classic outsider, as "Plum" Warner was part of the establishment. There is a revealing story of a preparatory school match in which Jardine captained Horris Hill and G.O. "Gubby" Allen captained Summer Fields, the smart Eton-feeder in Oxford. Both boys behaved just as they were to behave as adults and they obviously loathed each other on sight, a mutual hatred which endured until Jardine's early death in a Swiss clinic when in his fifties. He smoked a pipe which probably contributed to his fatal lung cancer.

That early prep school match is instructive. Allen and the cricket master, Mr. Alington, were determined not to lose. Christopher Hollis, later a Member of Parliament and a publisher, blocked his way to 18 runs in two hours and when the school was finally all out, Horris Hill had only twenty minutes left in which to score the runs. Unsurprisingly they failed and Jardine was in tears. The iron had entered his soul, even if it had not been there already.

That was 1914. Years later Jardine wrote a chapter on Test matches for the *Lonsdale Book of Cricket*, which I won as a prize at *my* prep school in 1955. Jardine quoted a school coach with evident approval. Jardine had yet to take his MCC/England team to Australia let alone his subsequent side to India. But the book was there for all to read and if anyone doubted the captain's hard-nosed attitude to Test cricket they had only to read his chapter on the subject in the Lonsdale book.

Consider this: "A great school coach, when speaking of the school match of the year, was wont to preface his remarks by saying, "these contests are second only to the battle of Waterloo!"

Jardine appears to approve and Horris Hill against Summer Fields would seem to fit the bill. In his case the child was father to the man and he tended always to play hard. The result seemed to be important. Not for him "It matters not who won or lost but how you played the game". You played the game to win; otherwise there was no point.

The article is interesting and anyone reading it should have been under no illusions about the sort of captain Jardine would turn out to be. You get a sense of him earlier in the book to which he also contributed two pieces on "Batsmanship". "We assume he means business", he says of the batsman, "Let him look as if he did so then. This does not necessitate looking like a cross between a tiger about to spring and a Captain of Industry signing his income-tax cheque – only let the batsman look alert, be braced as to his body, and concentrated on the business in hand." He is also photographed demonstrating "The Correct position as the bowler starts his run up to the wicket". Even the assumption that there is or was a "correct" position is interesting. In cricket matters, and certainly when it came to batting, Jardine was a great believer in "right and wrong". In the photograph he is, naturally, wearing his favourite Harlequin cap. He is facing the bowler with a two-eyed stance, watchful and defiant. He is tall, lean with a face that you would best describe as raw-boned, marked by a large aquiline nose and a strong jaw. He is wearing "proper" gear – an unbuttoned silk shirt, rather baggy cream flannels. His sleeves are rolled-up, his forearms bare and unprotected, gloves carry a lot of spikey rubber and the bat, apparently unmarked by maker's advertisement, looks old and trusty. He is emphatically not a person one would much like coming in to bowl at because he looks quite good (he was) and very serious. He evidently means business.

This is what shines through his piece on "Test match cricket". He is "concentrated in mind on the business in hand." And Test cricket, in particular, is obviously much more than a game. "This, one feels, is the real thing with the gloves off while it lasts. Clay pigeons are after all no substitute for the twelfth of August."

It is this seriousness which characterises the article and epitomises the man himself. He believed that international cricket was unlike any other form of the game and by international cricket he meant cricket between England and Australia. No other country is even mentioned and his admiration for Australia and the country's cricketers seems to know no bounds. "They have little to learn and much to teach" he tells us, adding that the list of the possible lessons "could be prolonged almost endlessly".

The greatest of all Australian lessons, however, was that they always played for a result. This was because in Australia matches continued until one or other side prevailed. In England this was not the case and time came into the equation. This meant that in sixty-seven matches played in Australia all but two had ended with a proper result and in only two early games was there a draw. Thus, argues Jardine "The Tests as experiments have been successful in nearly every case." In poor benighted England, however, fifty-two "Tests" had been played and "in twenty-three cases, or nearly 50 per cent, the experiment has been a failure or the result negative."

In other words the only really serious cricket for an Englishman (or a Scot such as Jardine) was a game played to the final conclusion. Such a game was played against Australia and Jardine was about winning. Nothing else mattered. As for Australian crowds, which he was supposed to hate – or come to hate – he said "With the exception of the Manchester crowd, which in the author's opinion has no superior, Australian crowds are better judges and keener critics of the game than most English crowds." However, he adds a caveat, saying that "it will be a thousand pities if a generation is allowed to grow up in Australia which allows a well-earned reputation for sound criticism and fair play to be discounted by partial and unintelligent barracking".

It should be noted here that "barracking" means one thing in England and quite another in Australia. In 'English' English it means general abuse but in Australia its meaning is necessarily partial. Thus "I barrack for the Crows" is an indication of support. In England it means indiscriminate jeering. Interesting, too, that Jardine who was widely regarded as a southern toff and a bit of a softy, should have singled out the Old Trafford crowd for special approbation. He would have been appalled to find that modern Test cricket has been removed from Lancashire and is now being played, in, of all places, Glamorgan.

Let it not be thought either that Jardine had no sense of humour.

"Some may not know the story of the Englishman fielding in the deep when a high catch was hit out to him", he writes, "In the momentary silence which nearly always follows such an event, he heard a voice behind say, 'Drop it – drop it, and I'll let you kiss my sister!'

"Fortunately perhaps for the English team's sake he was a cautious fellow, as he said to himself, 'I hadn't seen his sister!'"

Even allowing for the distance in time this may not seem like a particularly good joke, but it was a joke all the same, and a joke told by Jardine.

The rest of the team were, in alphabetical order, A.H. Bakewell, C.J.Barnett, E.W. Clark, C. H. Elliott, R.J. Gregory, J.H. Human, James Langridge, W.H.V. Levett, C.S. Marriott, A. Mitchell, M.S. Nichols, L.F. Townsend, B.H. Valentine, H. Verity and C.F. Walters. This made it a good team but not a great one and the only member of it who would now be in contention for an all-time England eleven would be the spin-bowler, Hedley Verity.

Verity, a thorough-going Yorkshireman, became a casualty of the Second World War. A Captain in the Green Howards, he was observed waving his revolver as he disappeared into the smoke on the island of Sicily in 1943. He led his company bravely through burning cornfields towards a German occupied farm-house urging them to "keep going" even after being wounded with a direct shot to the chest. The last his men saw of him as they retreated was of their stricken leader prone in front of the burning corn as his batman cradled his head in his arms. He died a few days later of his wounds as a prisoner-of-war in Caserta.

Verity was a phenomenon. He twice took all ten wickets in a match. The first time was at Headingley in 1931 against Warwickshire, who had earlier turned him down after a trial at Edgbaston. Those wickets cost him 36 but a year later on the same ground he took all ten against Nottinghamshire for just ten runs. This included a hat-trick, part of a fifteen ball spell in which he took seven for three and another spell when he bowled 113 balls without conceding a single run. They remain the finest bowling figures ever recorded and the fact that the wicket was a rain-affected "sticky" is only a marginal blemish.

He was the only member of the "Bodyline" tour to make the journey to India and although he disapproved of his tactics, he was ever-loyal in his support of his captain. Jardine returned the compliment, saying that Verity had "the oldest head on young shoulders in England". His second son was named after Jardine – the first having been named after his great precursor and mentor, Wilfred Rhodes. Despite the fact that the series was won with fast-bowling, Bradman, the pre-eminent batsman of that, or any other era, considered him his most fearsome opponent. "I could never claim to have completely fathomed Hedley's strategy" he wrote, "for it was never static or mechanical." In the famous Test at Lord's in 1934 – the only one at cricket's HQ when England beat Australia during the whole of the 20th century, Verity had Bradman twice and on one glorious June day took no less than fourteen Australian wickets.

The modern bowler he most resembled seems to have been Derek Underwood who, like Verity, bowled a little faster than most classic left-arm spinners. On the very last day of peace, in 1939, Yorkshire played Sussex at Hove in a benefit game for Jim Parks. They skittled the home side out for 33 on a drying pitch. Verity took seven for nine in six overs and bowled the last ball in County Cricket before the Second World War. It proved to be his own last also.

In his obituary *Wisden* recorded: "The balance of the run up, the high ease of the left-handed action, the scrupulous length, the pensive variety, all proclaimed the master. He combined nature with art to a degree not equalled by any other English bowler of our time. He received a handsome legacy of skill and, by an application that verged on scientific research, turned it into a fortune. There have been bowlers who have reached greatness without knowing, or perhaps, caring to know just how or why; but Verity could analyse his own intentions without losing the joy of surprise and describe their effect without losing the company of a listener. He was the ever-learning professor, justly proud yet utterly humble."

Fred Bakewell was one of the five *Wisden* Cricketers of the Year in the 1934 edition of the annual. Three of the others – Nichols, Townsend and Walters – were also members of the touring party to India with the quintet being completed by the West Indian batsman, George Headley, also known as "the black Bradman".

Bakewell, an opening batsman, was one of the class acts in a generally rather poor Northamptonshire team and he completed a thousand runs for the side eight times before 1936 when he suffered a horrific road accident immediately after completing a scintillating double century against Derbyshire. Earlier in 1933 he had made 107 in a Test match against the West Indian tourists. He was in his mid-twenties and a cricketer of unusual promise. After the road accident in 1936 he never played serious cricket again. He died in 1981.

Charlie Barnett, the Gloucestershire batsman who played in twenty Test matches, made great friends of Hedley Verity on the tour. Verity said of his new friend, that he knew "of no other cricketer upon whom one could rely whatever the state of the match. He really was a 'rock' when the chips were down. Nothing seemed to flurry him." Barnett himself was a dashing opening bat and a natural crowd-pleaser. Like other Gloucestershire players of the 1930s he was eclipsed by that magnificent all-rounder, Walter Hammond, who went on the "Bodyline" tour but did not go to India. The year after getting back from the sub-continent, in 1934, however, Barnett outscored Hammond by 2,282 to 2,081 at almost double the average. This was unusual. That year he and Hammond put on 251 for the second wicket against Sussex at Cheltenham, Barnett's birthplace. It was also in 1934 at Bath that he made 194 against his county's west country rivals, Somerset, and hit eleven sixes – a total only equalled at the time by Nayudu, India's best player of the twenties and thirties who did the same while scoring a century against MCC at Bombay on the tour of 1926/27.

Edward Winchester Clark, commonly known like most Clarks as 'Nobby', (Army slang for clerks on account of their smart black 'nobby' clothing), was widely regarded as the fastest professional bowler in England apart from the phenomenal Harold Larwood. He had the misfortune, however, to bowl in a rotten Northamptonshire team that once went 71 games without a win, picked up eight wooden spoons while he was playing for them and who really only had one competent catcher – Fred Bakewell who habitually fielded at short leg. To cap this Clark was a more than usually clueless batsman who never scored more than thirty and managed an average of only six despite batting in 477 innings for Northants and carrying his bat in more than a third of them. His temperament was so fiery that in one season his county failed to re-engage him and he sulked off to League cricket. He came back for a single season after the war and despite his by then advanced age he was able to bowl as fast as anyone albeit in very short bursts. He was a fine example of natural ability dissipated by temperamental instability.

Charlie Elliott was a useful opening bat for Derbyshire but really came into his own after retirement when he became a Test match umpire. He stood in 42 Tests beginning controversially in 1957 when he turned down a number of quite plausible lbw appeals from Ramadhin against a resolutely padding-up May and Cowdrey. He ended in 1971 at Lord's when – through no fault of his – water leaked under the covers and allowed Derek Underwood to take thirteen wickets for only 71. He was also a good enough footballer to play for Coventry City for whom he also acted briefly as a caretaker manager in the fifties. He was an England selector in the seventies. In later life he ran a B & B in Nottingham, a popular haunt for itinerant journalists where Elliott, upright and implausibly dark-haired even in old age was a genial host. Born in 1912 he survived into his nineties and only died in 2004, the last survivor of Jardine's Indian team.

Bob Gregory played for Surrey from 1925 until the outbreak of the war and then returned, like so many of his generation, to the county side for a fleeting period in the forties. He never played for England but was a more than useful county player with 38 centuries to his name as well as 434 wickets. He was an outstanding fielder, usually in the deep, where he held over 300 catches.

John Human, the youngest member of the side, was still an undergraduate at Clare College, Cambridge and was to be the captain of the university in the summer of 1934. He played for Middlesex from 1935 to 1938 and took part in a memorable partnership with 'Patsy' Hendren against Surrey at the Oval. The two put on 285 in 210 minutes and Human scored 144, the biggest of his three centuries. Human also bowled modest leg-spin and was a nifty fielder. In 1935 he was one of Errol Holmes' team that played four "unofficial" Tests against Australia. Human was in the team for each match but they were not accorded Test status so a full England cap eluded him. On the ship he met the daughter of the Lord Mayor of Sydney whom he subsequently married. For the rest of his life he lived in New South Wales, pursuing a business career and broadcasting on cricket. He died in 1991 and rejoiced in the nickname, "Bouncer".

James Langridge came from a famous family of Sussex cricketers which included his younger brother John who opened the batting for the county and his son Richard who did the same in the 1960s. He was originally taken on as a batsman and scored 1,000 runs in a season on twenty occasions ending with 31,716 runs and 42 centuries. As a bowler he might conceivably have won more than his eight Test caps had he not been unfortunate enough to play at the same time as Hedley Verity who was a similar sort of bowler only better. Even so Langridge was top of the county bowling averages in four different seasons in the 1930s. In 1933, on his debut against the West Indies, he took seven for 56 in the second innings. His total of 1,530 first class wickets took him to 77th on the all-time list. This coupled with his 52nd position in the batting list ensured his place as one of the English game's most successful all-rounders. He did the "double" every season between 1930 and 1937.

William Howard Vincent Levett came from a Kentish farming family and had the misfortune to overlap with Leslie Ames and Godfrey Evans both of whom were famous England wicket-keepers who also played for Kent and both of whom were more successful batsmen even though "Hopper" was alleged to be a reasonably accomplished batsman who once scored 76. He played for the county from 1930 to 1947 while Ames played from 1926 to 1951. Evans, a younger man, was something of a protégé of Levett's and learned from him how to stand up to the slower bowlers and to cease behaving like a not-very glorified long stop. Of Levett's 475 dismissals, 195 were stumped and such was his athleticism that Frank Woolley, an accomplished slip-fielder used to grumble that he was losing his catching bonuses because of Levett's poaching. Most of his appearances for the Kent first team were standing in for Ames when he was playing for England or absent with back trouble.

More importantly though "Hopper", so christened by his ebullient skipper Percy Chapman because his family grew hops and he was personally responsible for allocating supplies to the local brewers, was the life and soul of the party. He liked a drink and he liked a joke. He famously bowled a bread roll at the Australians one year and dropped a celebrated catch in a Gentlemen and Players match causing both batsmen and the rest of the fielding side to collapse with helpless mirth. In another match he was so hung over that he completely ignored the first ball which went for four byes and then took an absolutely blinding catch off the second. "Not bad for the first ball of the match", he commented blearily. Educated at Brighton College he made his debut for the Public Schools against the Australians and was much-loved in the game.

It was his misfortune to play for the same side and at the same time as two of England's most famous keepers but the truth is that he lacked the temperament to be a truly great cricketer. He was too keen on having a good time and encouraging others to do likewise. He was a good man to have on tour, however, particularly out in India.

Charles Marriott learned his cricket at St. Columba's in Ireland and was a crafty leg-break and googly bowler as well as an effectively useless batsman who averaged fewer than five runs an innings. He won a blue at Cambridge and played briefly for Lancashire before landing a job as master-in-charge of cricket at Dulwich College, alma mater of that keen cricket writer P.G. Wodehouse who named his butler Jeeves, after a Warwickshire bowler. When term ended Marriott would hurry down to Kent where he would wheel away in support of the legendary "Tich" Freeman. Despite playing in necessarily truncated seasons Marriott still managed to take 463 wickets for just over twenty apiece. He was one of the veterans of the team, having been born in 1895, some five years before Jardine. Perhaps partly for this reason he was always known as "Father". In the Oval Test of 1933 he played against the West Indies and so bamboozled them that he took five for 37 in the first innings and six for 59 in the second.

Arthur Mitchell, the Yorkshire batsman who was appointed county coach at the end of the war, continuing in the job until 1970 by which time he was in his late sixties was probably a more naturally talented batsman than he allowed himself to appear. In 426 matches for his county he accumulated 19,523 runs including 44 hundreds and 98 half-centuries. "Accumulated" was the appropriate word, however, and although he was a naturally fine cutter of the ball he seldom allowed himself to demonstrate this facility, particularly after taking over from Percy Holmes as the county's opening batsman. In 1933 he made more than 2,000 runs for Yorkshire and hit four consecutive centuries. His nickname was "Ticker" because he had the unusual habit of talking to himself incessantly, particularly while batting.

Stan Nichols, the Essex all-rounder, was already a veteran in his early thirties but as a cricketer he was in his prime. He was also one of 1934's *Wisden* Cricketers of the Year and about half-way through the eight doubles – a thousand runs and a hundred wickets – achieved in the decade before the outbreak of the Second World War. Eight was the same number managed by the gargantuan Dr W.G. Grace himself. In 1935 Nichols was the hero in an epic win over Brian Sellars' majestic Yorkshire side in Huddersfield. Essex won by an innings and 204, dismissing the mighty white rose side for just 31 in an innings. It was the only county match Yorkshire lost all season. Nichols with his right-arm fast medium bowling took a total of eleven wickets for 54 and, batting left-handed scored 146. A useful man to have on one's side, he played fourteen Tests for England but was never quite able to match the other front line bowlers around at the same time such as Larwood, Bowes, Allen and Voce. For Essex though he was lethal and for some time he was regarded as the best all-rounder in English cricket.

Leslie Townsend came late to cricket and only did so after watching a memorable innings by George Gunn. He was a prolific batsman for unfashionable Derbyshire and was nominated a *Wisden* Cricketer of the Year after scoring a record number of centuries for them in 1933. This included a double century against Leicester at Loughborough. In his first year however Derbyshire failed to win a single match though they recovered to such effect that in the three years culminating in 1936 they finished third, second and ultimately first in the County championship. Townsend was also a bowler of just-below-medium-pace off-breaks who was pretty innocuous on good wickets but could be lethal on "stickies" and once took a "hat-trick" at Northampton. Towards the end of his career he played briefly for Auckland and later settled in New Zealand where he originally intended to ply his trade as a cabinet-maker but became, at Nelson, one of the country's most successful coaches. He died in 1990 at the age of 89.

Bryan Valentine became one of the game's great characters and was once described by Frank Keating in the *Spectator* as "purply faced", which he can't have been as a schoolboy at Repton where he won the Public Schools' tennis doubles in partnership with "Bunny" Austin, nor at Cambridge where he won a blue as a nippy inside forward in the soccer team. He also became a scratch golfer, won a Military Cross during the war, worked in the same City bank as another, younger Corinthian cricketer, Colin Ingleby-Mackenzie. He captained Kent in a variety of partnerships beginning with one with Percy Chapman in the thirties, was a stalwart of the Band of Brothers and in the sixties, President of the County. He only played in seven Tests but made two centuries and had an average of just under 65 which was more than double his batting average for Kent. He liked to bat fast and elegantly and regularly scored at around fifty runs per hour. The anonymous writer of his *Wisden* obituary said that "in a friendship of over fifty years I myself never saw him anything but cheerful and usually laughing". Like his fellow man of Kent he was a more than useful cricketer but also a very merry tourist off the field and guaranteed to have a good time and to hold his own in India.

Cyril Walters was secretary and captain of a poor Worcestershire side from 1931 to 1935 but was a Welshman from Neath Grammar School who played several years for Glamorgan without undue success. His annus mirabilis was probably 1933 for he hit nine centuries for his county and played in all three Tests against the West Indies. He followed with a successful time in India, cementing his position as a stylish opening bat, before being chosen as England vice-captain to R.E.S. Wyatt and even substituting as captain in one match.

His life at the top was, however, short-lived and he resigned the captaincy and secretaryship to concentrate on marriage to his wealthy wife. She predeceased him in 1976 and he went back to live out his last years in Neath. Everyone seemed to like him and to appreciate his courtly diffidence. His relationship with Jardine seems to have been ambivalent and he claimed never to have understood him properly partly because the captain always seemed to be walking around with a book under one arm. On one occasion also Jardine's uncle was formed up with some Indian officials at a reception, unmistakeable because he, like the England captain, sported the distinctive, large family nose. Jardine however cut his uncle dead and walked straight past him without a hint of recognition. Walters was dumbfounded.

The team was managed by Major Ricketts who seems to have disappeared without trace. It was a first-class side with some fine cricketers and some great characters but it was short of real international quality. Several of its members played Test cricket, but few apart from Jardine and Verity, achieved genuinely consistent success. However they were good enough for India and probably for most international sides of the 1930s but they wouldn't have lived with Australia. Derek Hodgson, writing years later in the *Independent*, said, unkindly, that touring teams to India in those days tended to be "much more amateur than professional".

This was unfair for Jardine's team contained several very able professionals among them Langridge and Mitchell. It also included some equally able and serious amateurs such as Hopper Levett and Bryan Valentine, who were very gifted sportsmen but also gentlemen of independent means and disposition. And there were a number in-between. For the most part, however, it was a very jolly team, capable of playing some good cricket. Unlike their predecessors in Australia they were excellent ambassadors and they seem to have been united; not least perhaps because they were not encouraged to take their game or themselves unduly seriously.

3

Home From Home

The team sailed on the RMS *Mooltan* which was the ship that had brought Jardine and his men home from the infamous 'Bodyline' tour of Australia a year earlier. She was a P&O liner, broad of beam, stately of manner with a tiny rudder which meant that she had a reputation for extreme steadiness and stability but lacked manoeuvrability. She was grand but not nippy.

The *Mooltan* was a symbol of that vanished age in which the denizens of the pink areas on the map conducted their wanderings around a world on which the flag never came down. She was named after one of the Punjab's great cities, now the sixth largest in the whole of Pakistan. A famous battle was fought there in the middle of the nineteenth century after which a clasp was awarded to attach to the Punjab campaign medal and, as the British won, the Punjab turned pink in 1849. The city, sometimes known as the City of the Saints, was said to be built on the point where Satan himself had come to earth. In cricketing terms it is best known as the birthplace of the burly and aggressive former Pakistani batsman, Inzamam-ul-Haq.

Everybody in those days travelled by ship and if you were heading out East you went with the Peninsula & Orient line aboard a vessel such as the *Mooltan* which plied her trade between the United Kingdom and Australia. On her maiden voyage in 1923, she left Tilbury on 5 October and arrived in Sydney on 21 December. The journey between London and Bombay, which was the destination of Jardine's party in 1933, took about a fortnight.

Throughout the first half of the twentieth century this was the way cricketers from England travelled when they went to play international matches against those who lived in the other pink areas in Africa, the Caribbean, the sub-continent or down under. Photographs of MCC touring parties tend to show groups of formally dressed men in suits, often with hats and frequently clutching lighted cigarettes. The distinction between gentlemen and players, or professionals and amateurs was not usually apparent. Formality of dress and the ubiquitous cigarettes and other tobacco products give an impression, often illusory, of homogeneity and togetherness. I remember Denis Compton explaining a similar photograph years later. He was, Denis told me, not a proper smoker. He had a cigarette in his hand because everyone else did. It was expected. There may have been a distinction between "gentlemen" and "players" but they appeared on deck as a team. They all wore suits. And they all smoked because that's what chaps did.

Their landfall was in a city transformed by the construction of the Suez canal into one of the great ports of the Arabian sea and the main entry into the Raj. The Portuguese took what were then a series of disconnected islands from a local Gujerati ruler in 1534 and then, a century later gave them to Charles II of England as a dowry when he married one of their own, the infanta Catherine of Braganza. In 1668 the king leased the islands to the East India Company in return for a rent of £10 a year.

This was the beginnings of a transformation. The Company had been in this part of the world since establishing a factory at Surat in 1618. In 1687 Bombay became the Company's headquarters in India but in 1753 it yielded that position to Calcutta. The rivalry between the two greatest cities of India continues unabated to this day.

The most significant part of that transformation came in the first half of the nineteenth century when a scheme called the Hornby Vellard brought about the amalgamation of all the separate islands of the archipelago into one integrated whole. In 1853 the sub-continent's first railway linked the city with the suburb of Thane which has become effectively a part of the whole. Today Mumbai is either the world's second largest city (to Mexico) or the fifth largest conurbation depending on which way you choose to look at it. When the *Mooltan* docked in 1933 Bombay was huge, important in every way and paradoxically a major symbol of British rule and a vital centre in the struggle for independence.

Even at sea Jardine displayed the obsessive attention to detail which characterised his ruthless victory in the Ashes series a year earlier. He even cabled ahead to Karachi where the first matches were to be played asking for details concerning the length of the matting wickets, the height of the sightscreens and the state of the outfield. This statement of intent was matched by a radio message from the legendary and evidently self-confident C.K. Nayudu who met the challenge head-on. "Wait until you meet me," he said, on air.

Jardine, typically, had no intention of doing any such thing. He may have been an amateur in fact, as his distinctive Harlequin cap and patrician manner suggested, but in his attitude, his attention to detail and, above all, his desire to win, he was a professional through and through.

Not that he was lacking in respect for the Indian cricketer who was, in the words of Ramachandra Guha, "the first Indian cricketer to be a popular hero, whose appeal transcended the barriers of caste, class, gender and religion". Nayudu had played one of the great innings in 1926 when he hit a world record eleven sixes out of a whirl-wind 153 in under two hours. After the game he was presented with a gold medal, a silver bat and a Triumph motor-cycle with sidecar. If he failed to give Ashes victor Jardine pause for thought it was not entirely surprising. He was a god in his own country.

Ramachandra Guha, a thoughtful writer, a former Marxist and a fully-paid-up intellectual academic as well as a cricket fan is interesting on Nayudu's place in the evolution of Indian cricket and, by what seems to Guha a natural and inevitable extension, Indian nationhood. Nayudu was, he concedes, something of a *pukka sahib*, and had he been English, would have been an amateur like Jardine. Nevertheless he was perceived, rightly, as an Indian and as the personification of Indian aspirations. As Guha puts it, "his batsmanship became a vehicle for the articulation of suppressed national feeling".

He was also something of a one-man-band, to such an extent that Jardine came to refer to his team's opponents as "C.K.Nayudu's roving circus". Altogether he played eleven times against the tourists, appearing in each of three Test matches as well as for the Governor's XI in Lahore, the Viceroy's XI in Delhi, an Indian XI in Calcutta, Vizianagram's team in Benares – the only time Jardine's team lost a game , his own central state in Indore, for the Central Provinces and Berar at Nagpur and Moin-ud-Dowlah's XI at Secunderabad. Ram Guha points out that, despite the Dodge limo that Holkar had given his "King of Outdoor Games", Nayudu travelled everywhere second class whereas the English all went first. He also makes the fair point that Nayudu was "pushing forty" at the time.

Many of the greatest Indian batsmen, past and present, have been beautifully elegant players, all wristy and sinuous. I once saw Gavaskar and Tendulkar take part in an opening stand of a hundred for their country in Tasmania, against Pakistan. They were a joy to watch but they played the game as if it were hockey or badminton. They were deft and elegant and time and time again the ball sped to the boundary propelled by shots which seemed effortless and had everything to do with touch and timing.

However Nayudu was unlike so many of his compatriots, as he was a mighty hitter. While other great Indian batsmen stroked the ball he was a great exponent of the 'long handle'. Guha heard stories of incredible blows into the Bairds Barracks, the Sagar Talkies, the Plaza Cinema and other far-away targets each involving "carries" of more than a hundred yards and each one accompanied by an apparently genuine congratulation to the bowler. He must have been insufferable but he was also wonderfully defiant and a fine example to his patriotic countrymen.

Even so this deification was relative for cricket was essentially a minority sport and widely perceived as a British invention and even an instrument to sustain British rule. Lord Willingdon, who had won a cricket blue at Cambridge and was a believer in the game's value in non-cricketing or extra-cricketing terms even went so far as to say that cricket was "one of the links that binds the British Empire together".

In Australia on Jardine's "Bodyline" tour it very nearly proved to be the undoing of that Empire and you could plausibly argue that in the old country's former colonies it was sometimes perceived as an instrument with which to beat – literally – its founder and the imperial ruler in far-away Britain. The Trinidadian Marxist, C.L.R. James certainly saw it that way and men like Sir Donald Bradman and Learie, later Lord, Constantine did much to promote the independence of the countries from which they came. In British India at the time, however, Lord Willingdon was the patron of Indian cricket and he and Lady Willingdon entertained the teams in the Willingdon Pavilion. When they did so the mid-day meal was described as "luncheon". It was that sort of world and cricket was part of it. Even Nayudu was a Major in the Army. The rank was a sinecure provided by his employer, the Maharaja of Holkar, and it carried no responsibilities beyond the playing fields. The fact that it was considered desirable even for someone as God-like as Nayudu is significant.

It is difficult now to be sure about Indian attitudes to Jardine's "bodyline" or "leg theory" tactics in Australia. The *Times of India* displayed an ambivalence which was probably true of the Raj Establishment just as it was true of much of the "Establishment" at "home" in Britain. "One cannot but sympathise with the feelings of the Australian team", the paper's leader writer opined, but "The treatment accorded to Jardine is indefensible". One correspondent said that "bodyline" could mean anything "from hitting batsmen on the head to leaving Pataudi out of the team." Another writer said, "If anyone really wants some 'fun' let him put his baseball kit on and come and play fast bowling in office cricket in the Bombay midden." The paper reported that "a comedy touch was provided by Jardine who elected to field at fine leg near the boundary; his appearance so near the crowd was greeted with mingled applause and derision. Apparently Jardine felt this, because he stayed only one over and did not return to the boundary." Another letter, from a doctor called Pavri describes Australian "squealing" as "absurd" and, taking the line that the former colony was behaving like "an ungrateful child", complained about "the unsportsmanlike spirit on the part of the

Australians who do not seem to take defeat in the right sporting spirit as they desire to retain the Ashes by any means."

My sense is that opinion in India was divided just as it was in the United Kingdom. As time passes it begins to look less unified even in Australia where there was a strong Roman Catholic group led by Jack Fingleton and Bill O'Reilly which didn't rate Bradman as highly as he and his admirers. This was further complicated by a split between Roman Catholics and Protestants. One cannot help but notice that even as England and Australia were fighting out one of the most vituperative Ashes series of all time an Indian team beat a European XI (a euphemism for British in this context) by an innings and 109 runs in Madras. As the *Times of India* noted in a rather pompous verdict, "The Europeans made a poor show in their second venture."

There was, at the time, comparatively little "needle" involved in even the three Test matches between India and England. Jardine did not have Larwood, Bowes, Voce or Allen so that even though he might have the edge when it came to fast bowling he did not have the attack which had made his tactics so effective the winter before in Australia. The only survivor of that exercise, apart from Jardine himself, was Verity, a spin-bowler. It was not unknown for Australians to become effectively English – Somerset's Sammy Woods is one obvious early example – nor indeed for an Englishman to assume an Australian identity – Larwood himself and Frank "Typhoon" Tyson – are obvious examples of English fast bowlers who terrorised Australian cricketers and then came to live among them. However there was never an Australian equivalent of men such as Ranji, Duleep or Pataudi – aristocratic Indians who became in so many ways more English than the English.

Jardine's MCC team was not a full-strength England team; nor was India, particularly without their brilliant Maharajahs, yet in the same class as Australia. So despite the occasional hostility engendered by Jardine and his cricketing behaviour in Australia the Indian cricket world seemed genuinely pleased to greet them.

The MCC tourists landed on Indian soil on 12 October. For Jardine it was a homecoming. This was his birthplace; his father had practised law there; his father, Jardine's grandfather, had done the same before him. Jardine himself had not been back for twenty years. There, among the ecstatic crowd, who almost swept away the *All India*, was the faithful servant who had carried him around as a baby. The MCC captain posed for photographs with his bearer; he spoke felicitously of his links with Bombay; he praised "this great Indian Empire"; he even quoted Kipling. In other words he didn't put a foot wrong. He was pleased to be back; the Indians were pleased to see him; and Willingdon and his staff could take pleasure in an immaculate public relations exercise. It was emphatically not like Australia. Here the natives were friendly and deferential. They behaved with proper respect for a gentleman, a product of Horris Hill and Winchester College, a graduate of Oxford University. There were no larrikins here and the deck of RMS *Mooltan* was light years away from the hill at Sydney.

4

Opening Salvos

After the welcome ceremonies in Bombay the party journeyed north to Karachi. They remained on board the *Mooltan* until disembarkation when Jardine and C.S. Marriott apparently stayed with the Commissioner as befitted their gentlemanly amateur status. In fact, the remainder included a number of players from a similarly privileged background. Ramachandra Guha, makes the contrast between Jardine and Marriott and the remainder of the team seeming to suggest that they were "workaday professionals". But this MCC team was rather light on "workaday professionals". Larwood not only injected real pace, he also brought a touch of real working class.

The tourists played six matches in what is now, after partition, the problematic and troubled Muslim country of Pakistan. Of these half dozen games only one was dignified with the epithet "first-class". Three of these games were played in Karachi, two in Lahore and one up on the frontier with Afghanistan in the city of Peshawar. Such matches would be unthinkable in this commercial, television, financially-obsessed era. They could be described as "warm-up games" or "flag-waving exercises" but whichever way you choose to look at them they were mismatches to an even greater extent than the more serious first-class matches or the three Test matches against the best that the sub-continent had to offer. Outsiders simply didn't usually penetrate as far as Peshawar.

The opening game was played somewhere in Karachi though exactly where is not recorded. Nor do we know who the umpires were nor even who won the toss. The opposition was provided by a scratch outfit called C.B. Rubie's XI, though Rubie himself did not play. He seems to have been good enough because he played for the city against the tourists a day or so later and he was good enough to turn out for a Sussex team that also included the famous Indian cricketer Duleepsinhji who remained in England during Jardine's visit.

An odd characteristic of those days was that a certain sort of grand, cricket-playing Indian, spent as much time as possible in the United Kingdom behaving in an almost parodical P.G. Wodehouse manner while the sub-continent was full of men such as Rubie – military people, members of the administrative class, privately educated at middle-ranking public schools with predictable attitudes. Fundamentally decent, blinkered, but now outmoded if they still exist. The class system was alive and well in the early 1930s and nowhere more so than in British India.

Rubie himself became a Lieutenant-Colonel and was selected to manage the 1939–40 MCC tour of India which was cancelled for obvious reasons though the unfortunate Rubie went in to hospital for surgery in November and perished under the knife. He normally kept wicket but did not take part in the match against "his" team, leaving the wicket-keeping duties to Abdul Aziz who stumped the two Kent amateurs Valentine and his fellow keeper, Hopper Levett. Walters, Barnett and Valentine all rattled up fifties in a first-innings MCC total of 292. In their second innings the tourists made 70 for 4; the home side managed just 99 all out in their first innings and 103 for 6. So although the two-day game was drawn it was a one-sided affair though Rubie's opening bowler, Harris, took five for 89 and one for eight in the second. For MCC Townsend had match figures of seven for 50.

The only first-class match in this part of the world was against the province of Sind, whose nineteenth century conquest by General Napier, was famously reported in a coded telegram consisting of one Latin word – *peccavi*. As every schoolboy would once have known this meant simply "I have sinned". It would have been intelligible to anyone with a conventional classical education which meant, in effect, the entire officer and gentleman caste of the old British Empire. It was not a particularly sophisticated code but effective in its day. Today it would have been virtually useless. Jardine would have understood immediately as would the "Gentlemen" in his team. They would have known some Latin, the "Players" less if any.

Some two thousand years earlier, the Greeks, under Alexander the Great, had conquered Sind which regarded itself as the cradle of the Indian nation. In an etymological sense it seems to have got its name from the river Indus which defines it but it is also the origins of Hindu, Hindi and indeed India itself. Karachi is and was its main city and a great port, providing an important entry into the sub-continent.

In Karachi the MCC team played on the ground of the Gymkhana club which was founded in 1886, had several thousand members and was originally designed for the white British ruling class and their families along the lines of similar clubs back home. The Hurlingham in South West London was probably the proto-type. Later famous for croquet, polo and lawn tennis the Hurlingham was originally a club for the shooting of live pigeon. Like its Karachi counterpart it was a classic case of *rus in urbe*.

The opening first-class game was also a useful work-out which MCC won by 91 runs with most of the stars performing more than satisfactorily. Jardine made a not out century in the club's first innings and Charlie Barnett top-scored with 122 before falling to Sind's only Englishman, J.G. Harris. Nobody else made many in the first innings but Jardine was still able to declare on 307 for five; the second innings was less successful even though Barnett made a half century but as the first innings lead was well over a hundred it really didn't matter too much. When it came to bowling, Verity had six for 46 in the first innings and another four in the second. In the first innings Hopper Levett caught both openers and also caught the Sind skipper and stumped Irani as well off the bowling of Verity for a duck.

The Sind side boasted the requisite local aristocrat in Abdul Khalik, heir to Sheikh Sahib of Mangrol whom he would succeed in 1941. He was a member of a serious cricketing dynasty that carried Sind to the 1932 final of the Moin-ud-Dowlah Gold Cup played in

Secunderabad, only to lose heavily to a team called the Freelooters. In Sind's first innings against MCC he top-scored with 37 before falling lbw to Marriott.

1933/34 Sind v Marylebone Cricket Club
Karachi Gymkhana Ground. October 21, 22, 23, 1933
MCC won by 91 runs

Marylebone Cricket Club
First innings

Mr C F Walters	c Palsetia b Irani	26
A H Bakewell	c Palsetia b Irani	10
A Mitchell	lbw b Mohammad Ibrahim	6
C J Barnett	lbw b Harris	122
Mr D R Jardine	not out	101
J Langridge	st D J Mobed b Naoomal Jeoomal	13
R J Gregory	not out	15
H Verity	}	
Mr W H V Levett	} did not bat	
Mr C S Marriott	}	
E W Clark	}	
Extras		14
Total (112 overs) (5 wkts dec.)		307

Fall of wickets   1/20, 2/41, 3/45, 4/235, 5/275

Sind Bowling

	O	M	R	W
Palsetia	22	4	53	0
Harris	21	6	43	1
Irani	33	7	112	2
Mohammad Ibrahim	26	6	50	1
Naoomal Jeoomal	4	0	15	1
Gopaldas	5	1	14	0
B J Mobed	1	0	6	0

Sind
First innings

B D Shanker	c Levett b Verity	12
Naoomal Jeoomal	c Levett b Clark	30
Abdul Khalik	lbw b Marriott	37
M A Gopaldas	c Gregory b Verity	34
M J Mobed	c Jardine b Verity	20
J G Harris	lbw b Verity	1
S M Palsetia	b Clark	17
C Aste	c Levett b Clark	2
D J Mobed	b Verity	11
Mohammad Ibrahim	not out	18
S K Irani	st Levett b Verity	0
Extras		7
Total (78.3 overs)		189

Fall of wickets 1/40, 2/55, 3/108, 4/134, 5/139, 6/152, 7/157, 8/161, 9/177, 10/189

Marylebone Cricket Club Bowling

	O	M	R	W
Clark	20	4	69	3
Barnett	6	1	17	0
Marriott	20	8	44	1
Verity	23.3	11	46	6
Langridge	9	4	6	0

Marylebone Cricket Club

Second innings

A H Bakewell	lbw b Irani	17
R J Gregory	c Khalik b Palsetia	0
C J Barnett	c Khalik b Harris	54
Mr C F Walters	c M J Mobed b Mohammad Ibrahim	26
A Mitchell	b Mohammad Ibrahim	3
J Langridge	b Palsetia	0
Mr D R Jardine	c D J Mobed b Mohammad Ibrahim	20
H Verity	b Mohammad Ibrahim	10
Mr W H V Levett	not out	0
Mr C S Marriott }		
E W Clark }	did not bat	
Extras		10
Total (34.4 overs) (8 wkts dec.)		140

Fall of wickets   1/5, 2/42, 3/98, 4/102, 5/108, 6/137,
                        7/140, 8/140

Sind Bowling

	O	M	R	W
Palsetia	12	2	41	2
Harris	11	1	38	1
Irani	6	0	32	1
Mohammad Ibrahim	5.4	1	19	4

Sind

Second innings

B D Shanker	c Gregory b Langridge	19
Naoomal Jeoomal	lbw b Verity	2
Abdul Khalik	c Barnett b Verity	6
M A Gopaldas	lbw b Clark	7
M J Mobed	c Bakewell b Langridge	60
C Aste	b Langridge	6
S M Palsetia	c Levett b Barnett	33
J G Harris	b Verity	3
D J Mobed	c and b Marriott	9
Mohammad Ibrahim	c Bakewell b Verity	20
S K Irani	not out	0
Extras		2
Total (51 overs)		167

Fall of wickets 1/13, 2/19, 3/28, 4/70, 5/80 6/121, 7/135, 8/145, 9/148, 10/167

Marylebone Cricket Club Bowling

	O	M	R	W
Clark	7	1	21	1
Barnett	6	1	22	1
Marriott	15	7	52	1
Verity	19	10	35	4
Langridge	4	0	35	3

5

Cricketing Grandees

Stumps were drawn in Karachi on 23 October and MCC did not play first-class cricket again until 9 November when they took the field against Southern Punjab in Amritsar. Before then, however, there were three second-class games — one up in Peshawar at the gateway to the Khyber Pass into Afghanistan and a couple in the city of Lahore. In Lahore they first encountered the ubiquitous Nayudu who scored 116, but fared less well as a bowler, conceding 78 runs without taking a wicket. Nayudu seems to have scored his runs with characteristic aplomb and Ramachandra Guha quotes one witness's impressions. They are eloquent testimony to his vision of cricket as a political instrument.

"Every sixer hit by 'C.K.' wrote Prem Bhatia, in a book published more than half a century later, "was as good as a nail in the coffin of the British Empire . . . we madly cheered each shot past the boundary not only as a cricket performance but also as an assertion of our resolve to throw the British out of India."

In Lahore they also attended a party in the famous Shalimar Gardens now a UNESCO World Heritage site.

The Amritsar match was played on the Gandhi Sports Complex which was only completed earlier in the year. The Mahatma himself was no cricketer but he was already much in evidence, staging hunger-strikes, provoking hostile leaders in the establishment-supporting *Times of India* and generally being a thorn in the flesh of Lord Willingdon's administration.

Amritsar was at the time one of the most important cities in a united Punjab. The province is now divided with Amritsar being firmly in the southern, Indian, Hindu, non Muslim half. It is famous as being the home of the Golden Temple, apparently the most visited site in the whole of India, including the Taj Mahal. Amritsar actually means "Lake of the Holy Nectar" but I associate it with the massacre of 1919 when British troops under the command of General Dyer killed many Sikhs. As such it has become, for me, a symbol of British repression and fearful knee-jerk violence.

It began in 1919 with the Rowlatt Act which, basically, allowed the British to lock up their Indian subjects without trial or any form of judicial process provided they were suspected of "sedition". It sounds like an ill thought out and predictable reaction to "terrorism". There was a series of one-day strikes called "hartals"; the British responded with force, killing some protestors as a result of which three British bank managers were murdered. This was when Dyer was called in. Some 20,000 Indians were holding an apparently peaceful demonstration in Jallianwallah Bagh when Dyer arrived with 150 armed men and gave the order to open fire. Hundreds were killed and many more injured. The incident gave much-needed impetus to Gandhi's campaign of civil disobedience, was sym-pathetically filmed by Richard Attenborough many years later and was denounced by Sir Edwin Montague, the Secretary of State for India as a "savage and inappropriate folly".

It is worth remembering that in 1984 when Mrs. Gandhi was Prime Minister the Indian Army conducted another act which looked horribly like a second "savage and inappropriate folly" and which led to more massacres and eventually to the assassination of Indira Gandhi herself by her Sikh bodyguard. Thousands of innocent people lost their lives. So the Golden Temple is not just a very beautiful and very holy place, it is a site tainted with bloodshed and bigotry.

When Jardine's men arrived to play cricket in the city, General Dyer's massacre had taken place less than fifteen years earlier. It must have been a vivid memory for many; the area must have been full of Sikhs who lost loved ones during the violence, and the Mahatma, the incident's main beneficiary, was still actively pursuing his nationalist campaign against a government under Willingdon which seemed to many as blockheaded as Dyer. Indeed that sort of fearful, wrong-headed imperialism, could be said to be typical of parts of the regime. And there would be those who thought the world of cricket with its majors, its Maharajahs and the MCC touring team, was part of the same establishment. I think that would be a gross over-simplification but it would have been a point of view and not altogether an unpopular one.

Southern Punjab, the home team in Amritsar, were captained by Amarnath, who made a century in the first innings. Amarnath was still only twenty-one, and was to become the most significant player of his generation. He was to make his mark later on and was to become the first captain of a united post-partition India. He was born and brought up in Lahore but, as a Hindu, fled during the riots that accompanied partition and settled in India. He was one of the all-time great players but at this moment he was just embarking on his scintillating career.

In 1933 the most significant players in the Southern Punjab side were the Maharaja of Patiala and his son the Yuvraj. The elder Patiala captained the Indian cricket team which toured England in 1911, presented the Ranji Trophy, the most significant prize in Indian cricket and a memorial to the incomparable "Jam Sahib", and was a member of MCC. The Yuvraj was his heir and succeeded him in 1938 when the Maharaja died while not yet fifty. The 66 which the Yuvraj made in a century partnership with his captain was his highest score so far in first class cricket and he went on to play in just one Test match.

The Maharaja of Patiala, as we have seen, was almost impossibly grand, and after Amritsar his home state was the tourists' next destination. At home he not only showed Jardine and his team the fabulous collection of jewellery that was his pride and joy but also entertained them to various extra-mural jollities. "Nobby" Clark shot a cheetah and the rest of the players chipped in with deer and partridge. In between the fun they also managed to play cricket but the emphasis was on hospitality, lavish as only a Patiala could manage.

The Patialas generally, were of a completely different caste to practically everyone else. There is still, for instance something called the "Patiala Peg" which still surfaces in modern guide books to

India, even trendy ones such as *Lonely Planet* from where I derive my information on the notorious "Peg". Some time in the early 1900s apparently Patiala challenged the Viceroy and his team to a tent-pegging competition. This odd modernish take on jousting involved galloping horses, spears and tent pegs. It is peculiar to the sub-continent. Typically Patiala invited his opponents to drinks the night before. The drinks offered were far larger than usual and next morning Patiala also tampered with the tent pegs, making his own larger and the Viceroy's smaller. After Patiala's predictable and unfair victory the Viceroy's men complained and an affable Patiala apologised by explaining disarmingly that in his state the hospitality was such that pegs of whisky were always much larger than elsewhere. From that day disproportionately serious glasses of whisky have always been known throughout India as "Patiala Pegs". It was that sort of place and the Maharaja was that sort of chap.

Thanks largely to Amarnath and the Yuvraj, (the Maharaja was run out when he had scored 22), Southern Punjab made a respectable 264 but were still almost two hundred behind when Jardine, who did not bat, declared the innings closed at 450 for seven. In their second innings the Southern Punjab made an even more respectable 103 for one wicket but they took more than fifty overs to do so and the match petered out to a tame draw.

1933/34 Southern Punjab v Marylebone Cricket Club
Ghandi Sports Complex Ground, Amritsar. November 9, 10, 11,
1933
Match drawn.

Southern Punjab
First innings

Qamaruddin Butt	b Clark	0
L Amarnath	c Valentine b Clark	109
S. Wazir Ali	b Clark	3
Prithvi Raj	c Barnett b Nichols	0
The Yuvraj of Patiala	b Clark	66
The Maharaja of Patiala	run out	22
Nazir Ali	b Nichols	22
Mohammed Saeed	c Barnett b Verity	26
Ghulam Nabi	b Nichols	0
Barkat Ali	b Nichols	0
Mohammed Nissar	not out	6
Extras		10
Total (83.2 overs)		264

Fall of wickets   1/1, 2/9, 3/12, 4/146, 5/209 6/209,
                     7/237, 8/238, 9/238, 10/264

M. C. C. Bowling

	O	M	R	W
Clark	22	7	58	4
Nichols	20	1	87	4
Townsend	6	1	15	0
Verity	17.2	3	48	1
Human	8	2	21	0
Langridge	5	1	19	0
Barnett	5	2	6	0

M. C. C.

First innings

C F Walters	c Nazir Ali b Ghulam Nabi	86
J Langridge	c Amarnath b Prithviraj	32
L F Townsend	retired ill	93
C J Barnett	b Nazir Ali	39
Mr J H Human	b Ghulam Nabi	48
Mr B H Valentine	lbw b Nissaar	75
M S Nichols	c Prithviraj b Ghulam Nabi	55
Mr W H V Levett	not out	8
E W Clark	b Prithviraj	0
H Verity	not out	0
Mr D R Jardine	did not bat	
Extras		14
Total (110 overs) (7 wkts dec)		450

Fall of wickets   1/83, 2/153, 3/218, 4/295, 5/426,
                     6/443, 7/449

Southern Punjab Bowling

	O	M	R	W
Nissar	24	2	96	1
Nazir Ali	29	2	119	1
Ghulam Nabi	30	5	105	3
Barkat Ali	6	1	24	0
Prithviraj	21	1	92	2

Southern Punjab
Second innings

S. Wazir Ali	c Levett b Langridge	63
Prithvi Raj	not out	33
Qamaruddin Butt	}	
L Amarnath	}	
The Yuvraj of Patiala	}	
The Maharaja of Patiala	}	
Nazir Ali	} did not bat	
Mohammed Saeed	}	
Ghulam Nabi	}	
Barkat Ali	}	
Mohammed Nissar	}	
Extras		7
Total (50.4 overs) (1 wkt)		103

Fall of wickets   1/103

M. C. C. Bowling

	O	M	R	W
Clark	4	1	9	0
Nichols	7	1	14	0
Verity	5	4	1	0
Human	7	0	27	0
Langridge	9.4	5	8	1
Barnett	13	8	21	0
Valentine	5	1	16	0

The following day, 12 November, the Patialas, father and son, resumed hostilities on their own ground, the Dhruve Pandove Stadium in Patiala itself. MCC batted first and were all out for 330 with Jardine top-scoring on 80. Patiala's leading wicket taker was the Australian all-rounder Francis Tarrant who took four for 101. Tarrant was often considered to be the best cricketer never to win an international cap. In ten years playing for Middlesex before the outbreak of the First World War he did the double six times. He took nine wickets in an innings on five different occasions and in 1914 shared a second innings stand of 380 with J W Hearne for Middlesex against Lancashire. That same year he scored 250 not out against Essex at Leyton. In 1933 Tarrant was the Maharaja of Patiala's 'hired assassin'.

Almost half the Patiala side's 335 for 6 were scored by S. Wazir Ali, an elegant and forceful right-handed batsman destined to play permanent second fiddle to his great rival C.K. Nayudu, without much doubt, the best and most famous Indian cricketer of the day. Wazir Ali resented Nayudu who consistently up-staged him. As a Muslim he fled to Pakistan after partition in 1947 and died there in penury only three years later, after a routine operation for appendicitis. He was just 47 years old.

Although the match was scheduled to last four days it came to a conclusion with the home side five runs ahead with four wickets standing. Once again the Indians scored far slower than the visitors – an indication perhaps of the relative seriousness with which the teams were taking the games.

1933/34 Patiala v Marylebone Cricket Club
Baradari Ground, Patiala. November 12, 13, 14, 15, 1933
Match drawn.

Marylebone Cricket Club
First innings

A Mitchell	b Tarrant	59
A H Bakewell	b Nazir Ali	12
R J Gregory	lbw b Nazir Ali	0
C J Barnett	c Wazir Ali b Tarrant	39
Mr D R Jardine	b Irani	80
Mr B H Valentine	b Nissar	24
Mr J H Human	c and b Tarrant	47
J Langridge	c Gopaldas b Tarrant	34
H Elliott	lbw b Privthi Raj	8
Mr C S Marriott	c Nazir Ali b Privthi Raj	8
E W Clark	not out	4
Extras		15
Total (101.2 overs)		330

Fall of wickets   1/35, 2/35, 3/96, 4/154, 5/215,
                   6/241, 7/284, 8/309, 9/321, 10/330

Patiala Bowling

	O	M	R	W
M. Nissar	21	5	73	1
Nazir Ali	18	3	48	2
Irani	10	1	40	1
Tarrant	28	2	101	4
Gopaldas	17	4	37	0
Prithvi Raj	7.2	3	16	2

Patiala

First innings

S Wazir Ali	c Barnett by Langridge	156
Prithvi Raj	c Bakewell b Clark	1
L Amarnath	c Elliott b Clark	53
S Nazir Ali	st Elliott b Langridge	13
The Yuvraj of Patiala	c Mitchell b Langridge	37
Lall Singh	c Jardine b Gregory	46
M A Gopaldas	not out	13
F A Tarrant	not out	2
The Maharaja of Patiala }		
Mohammad Nissar }	did not bat	
S K Irani }		
Extras		14
Total (156 overs) (6 wkts)		335

Fall of wickets   1/1, 2/80, 3/117, 4/200, 5/313, 6/325

Marylebone Cricket Club Bowling

	O	M	R	W
Clark	41	16	82	2
Barnett	11	1	30	0
Marriott	44	11	86	0
Langridge	40	15	67	3
Gregory	9	2	19	1
Mitchell	2	0	5	0
Human	8	2	27	0
Jardine	1	0	5	0

The identity of one of the umpires is now unknown, but the other was the Bishop of Lahore. It was typical of Patiala to rope in a Bishop as umpire. It was typical of the man's style. The Bishop in question was the Rt. Rev. George Barne who had been appointed a year earlier and continued in the see until 1949. He was born in Jamaica and educated at Clifton College and Oxford University. He played some cricket at Somerset when in his twenties.

Christianity was not, however, what one associated with the hedonist, polygamous Maharaja and it is perhaps unsurprising that the two teams only managed just over 250 overs in a scheduled four days' play.

When the Viceroy remonstrated with Jardine about his plans to include Patiala in his MCC side, Jardine did not reply but simply fiddled with his pipe. Lady Willingdon also had a go at the England captain. Ramachandra Guha, whom I know and greatly revere as the Indian game's outstanding historian, says that Jardine, vexatiously included Patiala in the team which played Delhi and Districts – a game which did not have first class status. The scorecard says, however, that it was the Yuvraj and not his father, the Maharaja, who played for Delhi. He made 54, whoever he was, and at this time the son was a better player than the father.

The Delhi batting was opened by someone called Brittain-Jones who made nine in the first innings and ten in the second. Can this have been the same man as "Britten Jones", the Viceroy's military secretary who managed the Indians' disastrous 1936 tour of England? Ram Guha says that 'Britten Jones' never played and had little interest either. If they are one and the same person, and the names seem suspiciously close, Guha is, for once, mistaken. The Jones fellow may have been villainous but he wasn't a complete duffer and he must have been at least marginally interested in the game. Jack Brittain-Jones, if it is he, was an Army Captain, a Commander of the Order of the British Empire and a useful club cricketer who played a handful of games in India as well as being a playing member of that club and also the Free Foresters and I Zingari. He certainly formed a disastrous partnership with his friend "Vizzy" on the later tour of England but he was a keen cricketer with at least some ability in the abstract.

Tom Longfield who batted at number three and made a duck and three eventually became President of the Calcutta Club, was a stalwart of the Band of Brothers where he played with the tourists' Bryan Valentine, played a number of games for Kent and took eight relatively cheap wickets when Cambridge University, for whom he won a blue, beat New Zealand by five wickets. He was captain of Bengal when they won the Ranji Trophy for the first time in 1939. G.E.B. Abell, the wicket-keeper, turned out regularly for Worcestershire and scored a couple of hundreds for them. Francis Rogers scored almost eight hundred runs for Gloucestershire. So the Europeans may not have been great players, but they were useful and most of them had first-class experience. Even so the MCC won by an innings and 133 runs and Captain Brittain-Jones was on the losing side.

6

Big Game

Neither Patiala nor his son eventually played in the game between the Viceroy's XI and the MCC which began on 21 November in Delhi. "Brittain-Jones" however, opened the batting just as he had done for Delhi. This time he made eight and six. Another double-barrelled European, Oswald Smith-Bingham, went in further down the order and made seven and three. He was an officer in the 17th/21st Lancers who were stationed in Meerut where they were based for seven years right up until the outbreak of the Second World War. The score-card can be deceptive. The wicket-keeper, who 'bagged a pair' in the match was G.E.B. Abell, secretary to the Viceroy, a job he retained after the war when he served Lord Mountbatten in a similar capacity. Despite his poor showing in this game he was a more than useful county cricketer who averaged over 25 for Worcestershire between the wars and scored two centuries for the county.

Jardine put out a strong team and the Viceroy's men were brushed aside by an innings and 208 runs. Verity took seven for 37 in the first innings and Nichols five for 14 in the second. MCC started with an opening stand of over a hundred between Walters and Mitchell and never looked back. Valentine made 145, Jardine 93 and he was able to declare on 431 for 8. In the first innings the Viceroy's XI made 160 and in the second a mere 63. These low scores were recorded despite the presence of the two leading Indian batsmen Wazir Ali and C.K. Nayudu. Between them however they made just 42 in the first innings and ten in the second when Nayudu was bowled by Nichols for a duck. No wonder Willingdon hated Jardine.

1933/34 Viceroy's XI v Marylebone Cricket Club
Feroz Shah Kotla, Delhi. November 21, 22, 23, 1933
MCC won by an innings and 208 runs

Viceroy's XI
First innings

S Wazir Ali	c Mitchell b Verity	12
J Brittain-Jones	c Mitchell b Verity	8
T C Longfield	c Mitchell b Langridge	0
C K Nayudu	lbw b Langridge	30
A L Hosie	lbw b Townsend	26
G E B Abell	lbw b Verity	0
F G Rogers	c Barnett b Verity	8
L Amar Singh	c Townsend b Verity	0
O C Smith-Bingham	c Jardine b Verity	7
S Mushtaq Ali	not out	18
Mohammad Nissar	st Walters b Verity	42
Extras		9
Total (76.2 overs)		160

Fall of wickets   1/18, 2/19, 3/23, 4/78, 5/80 6/90,
                         7/90, 8/95, 9/111, 10/160

Marylebone Cricket Club Bowling

	O	M	R	W
Nichols	16	7	32	0
Barnett	6	1	15	0
Langridge	20	10	42	2
Verity	25.2	12	37	7
Townsend	8	3	15	1
Human	1	0	10	0

Marylebone Cricket Club

First innings

Mr C F Walters	c Abell b Mohammad Nissar	65
A Mitchell	c Wazir Ali b Mohammad Nissar	59
H Verity	c Nayudu b Mushtaq Ali	7
L F Townsend	lbw b Amar Singh	1
C J Barnett	c Hosie b Mushtaq Ali	0
Mr D R Jardine	b Longfield	93
Mr B H Valentine	c Abell b Mohammad Nissar	145
J Langridge	not out	17
Mr J H Human	c Nayudu b Mohammad Nissar	10
M S Nichols	not out	3
H Elliott	did not bat	
Extras		31
Total (144 overs) (8 wkts dec.)		431

Fall of wickets   1/109, 2/132, 3/135, 4/135, 5/142
                                   6/358, 7/412, 8/422

Viceroy's XI Bowling

	O	M	R	W
Mohammad Nissar	34	7	89	4
Longfield	28	5	87	1
Amar Singh	41	17	68	1
Nayudu	16	3	52	0
Mushtaq Ali	25	4	104	2

Viceroy's XI
Second innings

S Wazir Ali	c Mitchell b Langridge	10
J Brittain-Jones	c Verity b Nichols	6
T C Longfield	b Nichols	3
C K Nayudu	b Nichols	0
A L Hosie	lbw b Langridge	19
G E B Abell	b Langridge	0
F G Rogers	b Nichols	1
L Amar Singh	b Nichols	0
O C Smith-Bingham	c and b Verity	3
S Mushtaq Ali	not out	7
Mohammad Nissar	c Valentine b Langridge	11
Extras		3
Total (31.3 overs)		63

Fall of wickets   1/9, 2/13, 3/18, 4/20, 5/20, 6/25, 7/25, 8/44, 9/48, 10/63

Marylebone Cricket Club Bowling

	O	M	R	W
Nichols	10	5	14	5
Barnett	3	1	6	0
Langridge	12.3	4	23	4
Verity	6	2	17	1

Ram Guha says that while the match was being played the Government shut down the Secretariat and the Legislative Assembly. He also makes the point that Lord Irwin, Willingdon's predecessor had been subversively keen on Gandhi. Willingdon, however, was made of more conventional stuff. He and his countess turned up and sat in the eponymous Willingdon pavilion, waved, smiled and enjoyed themselves. Guha quotes the gushing description from the *Times of India*, an account in which the one-sided cricket match is hardly mentioned. Instead the reporter draws attention to the members of Council, the various ruling Princes, a host of ladies in the "prettiest garden frocks" and all-in-all "one of the biggest crowds ever seen in India". There were endless motor cars, a band, generous applause, and, that evening, the Imperial Delhi Gymkhana Ball, attended by the Willingdons and "a huge crowd on the floor."

Guha is caustic about the propaganda value of the whole exercise. "Delhi in November", he sniffs. "The Viceroy and his lady in their proper place, and the Indians in *theirs.* Cricket was once more the means by which the permanence of British rule would be assured."

Certainly the scorecard does not tell the whole story for the rules stipulated that the ground staff were only allowed to roll the wicket for seven minutes. In the event they rolled for at least twenty. Jardine insisted on an apology which he eventually won but his biographer suggests that it was no coincidence that Nichols' bowling included "a particularly fiery spell of 45 balls, five wickets for 7 runs." The bowling was often short but the field-placing orthodox. This did not, apparently, prevent some spectators from shouting out 'bodyline!' Their anger was misplaced but understandable.

The Viceroy's team was a classic example of what was wrong with a certain sort of British attitude. Apart from Wazir Ali and Nayudu there were only three other Indians in the eleven and of the remaining six Europeans, one, O.C. Smith-Bingham was making his first class debut. Smith-Bingham made seven and three and did not bowl. The Viceroy's captain was A.L. Hosie, probably the best European cricketer in India. Hosie was a jute merchant who had been educated at Oxford and scored five centuries batting for Hampshire. In his best year, 1928, he made 1,213 runs for the county – over a hundred more than his captain Lionel Tennyson though less than half the total run up by Philip Mead who was, as so often, Hampshire's most prolific batsman. In India Hosie had the unusual double merit of being socially acceptable and useful at cricket. Most Europeans failed one or other of these tests.

Delhi hasn't always been India's capital and there have, in any case, been eight cities in the area during the last 2,500 years. Of these the British was arguably the grandest and certainly the latest and most short-lived. The previous seat of the Raj had been Calcutta but Calcutta was tricky and Bengal 'bolshy'. The British decided to build a brand new capital on which the sun would never set and commissioned their most favourite architect, Edwin Lutyens, to be the principal planner. The new city was conceived in 1911, inaugurated twenty years later and in 1947 the British departed leaving behind a divided Dominion.

After the one-sided game against the Viceroy's XI, the tourists moved to Ajmer for their next match against Rajputana which began on 25 November.

The ground where the match was played was and is part of the spectacular surroundings of one of India's grandest fee-paying schools. Mayo College was founded by the 6th Earl of Mayo who was Viceroy from 1869 to 1872. The original concept was that of a Colonel Walter and the first headmaster was another Colonel, Sir Oliver St. John. Another later Viceroy, the 1st Earl of Lytton, speaking to the boys in 1879, commended Colonel Walter's "very sensible report" which was that what Indian chaps most needed was an Indian Eton. Thus the school. "Ajmer", said the Viceroy, "is India's Eton and you are India's Eton boys."

Ajmer itself is now a city of just under half a million inhabitants and was once a place of some importance. One of the first meetings between the British, in the person of Sir Thomas Roe and the Mughals, personified by Jehangir, took place in Ajmer in 1616. Just over two hundred years later, after a long period of Scindia control, it was handed over to the British in 1818. There is a famous lake, Ana Sagar, formed in the twelfth century by damming the River Luni, which is flanked by a couple of parks, the Dault Bagh and the Subash Bagh and the town houses one of the most important places of Muslim pilgrimage in the whole of India. But, for the British, Ajmer is and was best known as the home of Mayo College.

The match itself was an extraordinarily low-scoring affair. MCC posted a modest 213 with the Rajputana opening bowlers Ramji and Azin Khan accounting for seven with all but one caught. Only Barnett scored more than 50. When they batted, however, Rajputana were bundled out for only 32 by Clark and Townsend who took five

apiece, the former for 10 and the latter for 16. The home side didn't
do much better in their second innings, managing just 74. Townsend
did most of the damage this time with seven wickets for 22. The
Indian aristocrat on this occasion was the Maharawal of Dungapur
who captained the side but was caught and bowled by Townsend for
a duck in the first innings and was lbw to the same bowler for five in
the second. Rajputana played two Europeans, Hancock and Hills,
but neither achieved anything of note. Jardine did not play and in his
absence the side was captained by Walters.

1933/34 Rajputana v Marylebone Cricket Club
Mayo College Ground, Ajmer. November 25, 26, 1933
MCC won by an innings and 107 runs

Marylebone Cricket Club
First innings

A H Bakewell	c Azim Khan b Murad	8
R J Gregory	c Hansraj b Ramji	9
L F Townsend	c Hansraj b Ramji	1
C J Barnett	c Ramji b Azim Khan	75
Mr B H Valentine	c Himmatsinhji b Azim Khan	34
A Mitchell	lbw b Ramji	4
J Langridge	b Attique Hussain	28
Mr C F Walters	c Hansraj b Azim Khan	0
Mr W H V Levett	c Azim Khan b Ramji	25
H Elliott	lbw b Hills	1
E W Clark	not out	7
Extras		21
Total (79 overs)		213

Fall of wickets   1/23, 2/24, 3/31, 4/120, 5/130,
                         6/151, 7/160, 8/191, 9/192, 10/213

Rajputana Bowling

	O	M	R	W
Ramji	23	8	53	4
Azim Khan	19	8	41	3
Murad	10	3	25	1
Hills	10	3	24	1
Attique Hussain	13	3	36	1
Hansraj	4	1	13	0

Rajputana
First innings

Ghulam Mohiuddin	c Gregory b Clark	1
Danmal Mathur	lbw b Townsend	7
Attique Hussain	c Langridge b Clark	0
Azim Khan	lbw b Townsend	0
Maharawal of Dungapur	c and b Townsend	0
Hansraj	b Clark	0
C P Hancock	c Barnett b Townsend	7
K S Himmatsinhji	not out	4
L Ramji	b Clark	0
J Hills	c Valentine b Townsend	8
K B Murad	c Barnett b Clark	2
Extras		3
Total (22.4 overs)		32

Fall of wickets   1/3, 2/3, 3/4, 4/4, 5/9, 6/13, 7/18,
8/19, 9/28, 10/32

Marylebone Cricket Club Bowling

	O	M	R	W
Clark	11.4	6	10	5
Barnett	2	0	3	0
Townsend	9	2	16	5

Rajputana
Second innings

Danmal Mathur	b Townsend	19
K S Himmatsinhji	c Mitchell b Clark	6
Maharawal of Dungapur	lbw b Townsend	5
Attique Hussain	c Gregory b Townsend	0
Hansraj	c Barnett b Townsend	1
J Hills	b Townsend	0
C P Hancock	lbw b Townsend	15
Azim Khan	b Townsend	6
Ghulam Mohiuddin	not out	8
L Ramji	c Valentine b Langridge	10
K B Murad	b Langridge	1
Extras		3
Total (36.2 overs)		74

Fall of wickets   1/11, 2/20, 3/20, 4/23, 5/23, 6/47,
7/53, 8/58, 9/69, 10/74

Marylebone Cricket Club Bowling

	O	M	R	W
Clark	8	2	19	1
Barnett	1	0	2	0
Townsend	17	9	22	7
Langridge	8.2	4	24	2
Gregory	2	0	4	0

In fact Jardine had taken time off to go and shoot tiger in Junagad. Guha adds an "h" to the end of the name and says that Jardine hired thirty beaters "to induce a lion to sweep past his Machan on a tree in the recesses of the Gir Forest". Junagad or Junagadh was, apparently, the last redoubt of the Asiatic lion. The captain spent three days up a tree waiting for a lion. Finally one came by and Jardine shot it dead and took the skin home.

In a 2005 survey the number of Asiatic lions was said to be 359, the result of serious protection and conservation. When "trophy-hunters" such as Jardine were at their zenith the lion population declined to as few as 15. Then, however, the local ruler declared them to be an endangered species and launched a programme for preserving them and enhancing their survival.

Jardine then moved on to Killeshwar in Nawanagar State, which used to be a favourite hunting ground of Ranjitsinhji, "The Jam Sahib", and possibly the finest cricketer India ever produced. Here he shot an eight foot panther which turned nasty and mauled a couple of bearers. The party ended at the Maconochie Club where the captain won a silver cup for general knowledge. A little later it was reported that "D.R. Jardine who has been on a shooting expedition is suffering from a touch of malaria. It is not serious, however, and he is expected here tomorrow by air." Later, when he did rejoin his men, the tigers had become lions.

From one school ground the touring party moved on to another, the Rajkumar College Ground at Rajkot where, on 30 November, they began a three day match against Western India. Jardine was still absent so Valentine captained the side in his place. The college is the alma mater of two of the greatest cricketers ever produced by India, Ranji and his nephew Duleep.

The Mahatma lived in Rajkot and his family home is now open to the public. The city itself now contains over a million inhabitants. It was once the capital of the princely state of Saurashtra and is now the second Gujerati City after Ahmedabad. Like so much of the world's largest democracy the vestiges of British rule linger on in a languid, half-affectionately remembered state and one of Rajkot's main tourist attractions is the Watson Museum and Library, a sort of higgledy-piggledy Gujerati take on the Pitt-Rivers Museum in Oxford. It is named after Colonel John Watson who was the political agent here between 1886 and 1889. His eclectic collection of antique bits and pieces is assembled under the austere and unsmiling gaze of the Queen-Empress Victoria.

Once again the result of the match was never seriously in doubt after the home side were bundled out, this time for 64 runs with Townsend taking seven wickets for 16. Even so events did not continue quite as might have been expected. MCC declared on 254 for five with Barnett top-scoring with 84. However the home side batted much more successfully in the second innings making 249. Verity who hadn't taken a single wicket in the first innings managed six in the second but conceded what was for him a large number of runs – 83. In their second innings MCC had a shock when they were reduced to 32 for five but in the end they knocked off the 60 necessary runs with four wickets to spare.

1933/34 Western India States v Marylebone Cricket Club
Rajkumar College Ground, Rajkot. November 29, 30, December 1, 1933
MCC won by four wickets

Western India States
First innings

N D Marshall	c Elliott b Nichols	1
R J O Meyer	b Clarke	0
O Manilal	b Townsend	3
Ganashyamsinhji	b Townsend	20
Hari Mali	c and b Townsend	2
Dr M S Gurtu	b Townsend	8
L Amar Singh	lbw b Townsend	8
The Jam Sahib of Nawanagar	c Mitchell b Townsend	0
L Ramji	b Nichols	12
V P Mehta	b Townsend	1
R S Pratapsinhji	not out	0
Extras		9
Total (21.3 overs)		64

Fall of wickets   1/1, 2/1, 3/20, 4/24, 5/32, 6/40,
                      7/40, 8/60, 9/62, 10/64

Marylebone Cricket Club Bowling

	O	M	R	W
Clark	4	1	6	1
Nichols	5	0	10	2
Townsend	7.3	1	16	7
Verity	5	0	23	0

Marylebone Cricket Club

First innings

A Mitchell	b Amar Singh	3
A H Bakewell	retired hurt	17
M S Nichols	b Meyer	52
C J Barnett	lbw b Ramji	84
L F Townsend	c Mehta b Ramji	26
Mr B H Valentine	run out	12
J Langridge	not out	23
Mr J H Human	not out	17
H Verity }		
H Elliott }	did not bat	
E W Clark }		
Extras	20	
Total (67 overs) (5 wkts dec.)		254

Fall of wickets   1/8, 2/120, 3/163, 4/207, 5/208

Western Indian States Bowling

	O	M	R	W
Amar Singh	19	2	62	1
Ramji	17	3	59	2
Meyer	10	0	32	1
Gurtu	8	0	38	0
Hari Mali	4	1	12	0
Pratapsinhji	9	0	31	0

Western India States
Second innings

V P Mehta	c and b Townsend	4
Dr M S Gurtu	c Barnett b Townsend	61
O Manilal	lbw b Verity	44
Ganashyamsimhji	c Barnett b Verity	13
N D Marshall	st Elliott b Verity	5
L Amar Singh	c Valentine b Townsend	41
R J O Meyer	c Barnett b Verity	18
Hari Mali	b Clark	26
L Ramji	c Nichols b Verity	6
The Jam Sahib of Nawanagar	b Verity	6
R S Pratapsinhji	not out	1
Extras		24
Total (79.4 overs)		249

Fall of wickets   1/16, 2/110, 3/130, 4/141, 5/145,
6/190, 7/232, 8/237, 9/244,
10/249

Marylebone Cricket Club Bowling

	O	M	R	W
Clark	18	7	29	1
Nichols	10	3	28	0
Townsend	21	5	65	3
Verity	26.4	6	83	6
Langridge	4	2	20	0

Marylebone Cricket Club
Second innings

A Mitchell	c sub b Amar Singh	2
J Langridge	lbw b Ramji	11
H Verity	c Meyer b Amar Singh	9
C J Barnett	c and b Ramji	0
L F Townsend	not out	22
M S Nichols	b Amar Singh	2
Mr B H Valentine	c Mehta b Amar Singh	9
Mr J H Human	not out	5
A H Bakewell	}	
H Elliott	} did not bat	
E W Clark	}	

Extras	0
Total 30.5 overs) (6 wkts)	60

Fall of wickets   1/9, 2/22, 3/22, 4/27, 5/32, 6/54

Western Indian States Bowling

	O	M	R	W
Amar Singh	15.5	5	41	4
Ramji	15	7	19	2

Western India played no maharajahs but were probably hindered by the presence of two fancy-hats, K.S. Digvijaysinhji who captained the side and K.S. Pratapsinhji. Both men were making their debut in first class cricket. They made seven runs between them and took no wickets. R.J.O. Meyer, the future headmaster of Millfield, opened the Western Indian's first innings but was bowled by Clark for a duck. Not that Meyer was a duffer. In 1936, batting for Somerset at Taunton, he made an unbeaten double century against Lancashire. Amar Singh, by contrast, who shook the visitors up in their second innings with four for 41 was a genuine class act whose fourth wicket in that unconvincing second innings was his two hundredth in first class cricket.

The captain returned for the next match against Jamnagar at the Ajitsinhji Ground played over two days at the beginning of December though it was curtailed at lunch on the second day when stumps were drawn so that the tourists could head off for Kilieshwar for a panther-hunting expedition. This was Duleepsinhji's home state and the great man sent a telegram of welcome to Jardine and his team. Mitchell who opened the MCC innings with Human had to retire hurt when he was struck on the jaw by a ball from Amar Singh. Amar Singh was lively and took six for 73. It was a low-scoring game with the home side making just 90 and 45 for 6, MCC got off to a nightmare start, losing three of their first four batsmen for single figure scores. They were rescued however by Walters who made 60 and Verity who finished on 28 not out, enabling them to declare on 151 for eight.

Jamnagar was also the former fiefdom of His Highness Shri Sir Ranjitsinhji Vibhaji Maharaja Jam Sahib of Nawanagar, known to everyone as Ranji or the Jam Sahib. He was probably the greatest cricketer India had ever produced but who played his cricket, like his nephew Duleep, for Sussex and England. Ranji was such an Anglophile that he made his Royal Band play *The Roast Beef of Old England* at state occasions. Even friendly British guests raised eyebrows at this vicariously patriotic enthusiasm. Jamnagar was, after all, a Hindu state where the eating of beef was strictly forbidden. Jardine and his men were made to feel thoroughly at home there, despite the belligerence of Amar Singh.

The next game was a serious affair at the Gymkhana Ground in Bombay against the eponymous home side. The Bombay Gymkhana was, like its Karachi counterpart, a Victorian foundation established in 1875 as part of an exclusive club which was, at first restricted to the British alone. For many years it was one of the great grounds of the sub-continent, hosting the Bombay Quadrangular Tournament as well as many international matches. In 1948, the Brabourne Stadium was built and became the prime Calcutta cricket ground. The ground was named after Lord Brabourne, the Governor of Bombay, who was offered the choice of money for the benefit of his sporting enthusiasms or immortality in the shape of a stadium named in his honour. He chose immortality. In the early seventies there was a dispute between the Cricket Club of India and the Mumbai Cricket Association over the allocation of tickets. As a result the Mumbai Association took umbrage and built another ground of their own, the Wankhede Stadium. This was recently refurbished for the World Cup of 2011. It has gates named after the local stars Polly Umrigar and Vinoo Mankad with eponymous stands called the Merchant (Vijay), the Gavaskar (Sunil), and the Tendulkar (Sachin). It is bizarre to have three such grounds within a short distance of each other in the south of the city but local rivalries clearly ran deep. Since 1948 no Test matches have taken place on the Gymkhana ground in the south of the city at one end of the Azad Maidan but it was here that Jardine's men performed.

Jardine went in at number five and made 102. He and Gregory who scored 148, put on 158 for the sixth wicket and MCC declared at 481 for eight wickets, a first innings lead of almost four hundred. In Bombay's second innings Vijay Merchant, the star of the home side made 67 not out in a much more spirited 191 for five wickets which saved the match but overall the tourists looked too strong for their opponents.

1933/34 Bombay v Marylebone Cricket Club
Gymkhana Ground, Bombay. December 8, 9, 10, 1933
Match drawn.

Bombay
First innings

C M Mehta	c and b Verity	17
S S Joshi	c Barnett b Nichols	2
L P Jai	c Jardine b Clark	1
S H M Colah	c Barnett b Clark	0
H J Vajifdar	c Barnett b Nichols	0
V M Merchant	not out	19
J P Havewallah	c Gregory b Verity	5
K R Meherhomji	c Walters b Marriott	21
R J D Jamshedji	c Gregory b Nichols	0
A A Hakim	st Levett b Verity	7
D S Talpade	run out	6
Extras		9
Total (35 overs)		87

Fall of wickets   1/6, 2/7, 3/7, 4/8, 5/35, 6/58, 7/58, 8/62, 9/77, 10/87

M.C.C. Bowling

	O	M	R	W
Nichols	9	2	21	3
Clark	11	5	13	2
Verity	11	4	25	3
Marriott	4	2	19	1

M.C.C.

First innings

Mr C F Walters	b Jamshedji	54
J Langridge	c Meherhomji b Mehta	66
L F Townsend	c Meherhomji b Talpade	30
C J Barnett	c Hakim b Jamshedji	23
Mr D R Jardine	c Hakim b Jamshedji	102
M S Nichols	b Jamshedji	1
R J Gregory	st Meherhomji b Jamshedji	148
H Verity	st Meherhomji b Jamshedji	49
Mr W H V Levett	not out	4
E W Clark	not out	0
Mr C S Marriott	did not bat	
Extras		4
Total (144 overs) (8 wkts dec.)		481

Fall of wickets   1/93, 2/144, 3/164, 4/191, 5/197,
                       6/355, 7/469, 8/478

Bombay Bowling

	O	M	R	W
Talpade	43	6	130	1
Vajifdar	25	7	84	0
Joshi	18	5	54	0
Hakim	4	0	26	0
Jamshedji	35	0	127	6
Havewallah	13	4	26	0
Mehta	6	0	30	1

Bombay
Second innings

C M Mehta	b Nichols	7
S S Joshi	c Barnett b Verity	36
S H M Colah	c Langridge b Verity	33
V M Merchant	not out	67
L P Jai	c Nichols b Langridge	13
H J Vajifdar	b Marriott	20
J P Havewallah	not out	7
K R Meherhomji }		
R J D Jamshedji }	did not bat	
A A Hakim }		
D S Talpade }		
Extras		8
Total (92 overs) (5 wkts)		191

Fall of wickets   1/8, 2/57, 3/115, 4/131, 5/182

M. C. C. Bowling

	O	M	R	W
Nichols	14	3	37	1
Clark	14	8	25	0
Verity	15	7	25	2
Marriott	19	10	44	1
Langridge	20	10	26	1
Townsend	8	3	24	0
Gregory	2	1	2	0

Several of the team who played in the first Bombay match also took part in a second two day match which did not attract first class status and was drawn. That left one rest day before the first, inaugural Test match and Jardine used it to accompany his father's former butler, Lalla Sebastien, to the Sewri cemetery where the old retainer wished to lay a wreath on his wife's grave. As Ramachandra Guha remarks in his history of Indian cricket, "What student or participant of

The MCC touring party on board RMS *Mooltan* en route to India.

MCC begin their 1st innings v. NW Frontier Province at Peshawar on the first grass pitch of the tour so far.

MCC and the Punjab Governor's XI before the match at Lahore.

C.F. Walters and the Maharaja of Patiala toss up before the match between MCC and Northern India at Lahore.

The MCC are welcomed at the Parsee Gymkhana in Bombay.

The second Test at Calcutta - Sleeping guards protecting the Test pitch.

The two captains, Douglas Jardine and Major C.K. Nayudu, before the second
Test match at Calcutta.

An invitation to dinner for C.F. Walters from the Viceroy on the first evening of
the second Test at Calcutta.

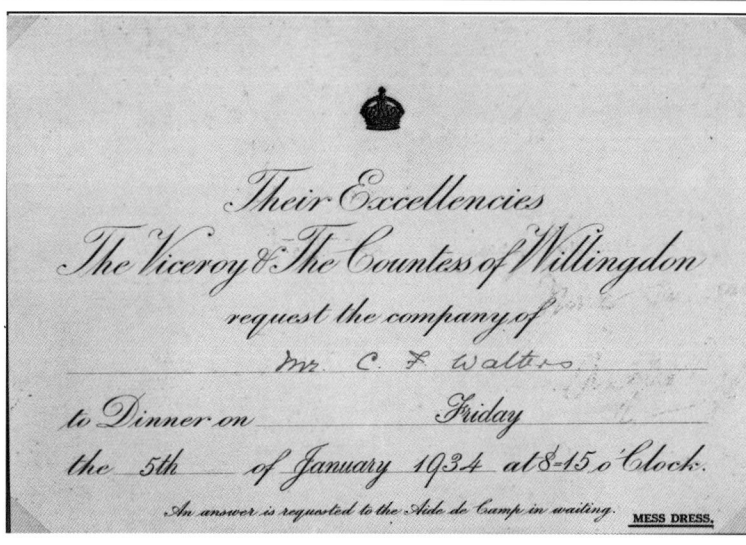

MCC versus Maharaja Kumar of Vizianagram's XI at Benares. Vizzy's XI are in the field. His palace is in the background.

MCC versus Maharaja Kumar of Vizianagram's XI at Benares. Vizzy batting in front of his palace.

C.F. Walters leads out the MCC against Central India at Indore. Daly's College is in the background.

The three Nayudu brothers, from left:- Major C.K., C.S., C.L.

Both teams before the match between MCC and the Nawab of Moin-Ud-Dowlah XI at Secunderabad.

Kaute Steward

Thursday, 8th March 1934.

GOVERNMENT HOUSE ENGAGEMENTS.

Date.	A.D.C.-in-waiting.	Time.	ENGAGEMENTS.
			MARCH
8 Thurs.	Capt. Gosling.	7 A.M.	Their Excellencies will visit the Buckingham and Carnatic Mills.
		...	Admiral Sir Victor and Lady Stanley arrive at Bombay.
		10-30 A.M.	His Excellency will see the Hon'ble Justice Sir Owen Beasley at Government House, Madras.
		11 A.M.	Legislative Council Meeting.
		2 P.M.	His Excellency will see the goods of Mr. Chunna Lall Indar Bhan Sadh at Government House, Guindy.
9 Fri.	Capt. Batt.	7-45 A.M.	English Mail leaves.
		8-30 A.M.	Mr. C. F. Walters (M.C.C. Team) leaves for Bombay. (Bombay Express—Central Station.)
		11 A.M.	Legislative Council Meeting.
		11-30 A.M.	His Excellency will see the Right Hon'ble V. S. Srinivasa Sastri at the Secretariat.
		12 NOON.	His Excellency will see Sir C. Sankaran Nair at the Secretariat.
		1-30 P.M.	Mr. E. J. Rowlandson comes to lunch.
		4-30 P.M.	Children of Deaf and Dumb School come to tea.
		8-30 P.M.	Dinner and Dance at the Adyar Club.
10 Sat.	Capt. Wright.	...	Legislative Council Meeting. (Voting on demands for grants.)
		...	Madras Races.
		5-45 P.M.	His Excellency will preside at the Annual Sports of the European Schools Athletic Association at the Doveton-Corrie Grounds.
		6 P.M.	Afternoon Dance at the Adyar Club.
		8-30 P.M.	His Excellency will dine with Colonel Stubbs and Officers of 2nd Battalion, the Suffolk Regiment, at the Mess, Fort St. George.
11 Sun.	Capt. Gosling.	11 A.M.	His Excellency will see Diwan Bahadur Sir Alladi Krishnaswami Ayyar at Government House, Guindy.
12 Mon.	Capt. Batt.	...	Legislative Council Meeting. (Voting on demands for grants.)
		11 A.M.	*Her Excellency will preside at the Annual General Meeting of the Countess of Dufferin Fund at Government House.*
		5-30 P.M.	His Excellency will preside at the Annual Meeting of the Madras Young Men's Christian Association. (Esplanade.)
		8-30 P.M.	Their Excellencies will dine with the Hon'ble Sir Mahomed Usman Sahib at the Freemasons Hall.
13 Tues.	Capt. Wright.	...	Legislative Council Meeting. (Voting on demands for grants.)
		11-55 A.M.	Air Mail leaves.
		12 NOON.	His Excellency will see the Inspector-General of Police at the Secretariat.
		12-30 P.M.	His Excellency will see the Chairman, Madras Services Commission at the Secretariat.
		...	Madras Races. (Provisional.)
		6 P.M.	M.M.A. Choral Concert "Messiah" at the Museum Theatre.
		8-30 P.M.	Dinner and Dance at the Adyar Club.
14 Wed.	Capt. Gosling.	...	Legislative Council Meeting. (Voting on demands for grants.)
		11-30 A.M.	His Excellency will receive a deputation from the Madras Landholders Association at the Secretariat.
		12 NOON.	His Excellency will see the Chief Secretary at the Secretariat.
		BETWEEN 5 AND 6 P.M.	His Excellency's Band plays at the Adyar Club.
		6 P.M.	Afternoon Dance at the Adyar Club.
		8-30 P.M.	Dinner Party at Government House, Guindy.
15 Thurs.	Capt. Batt.	...	Legislative Council Meeting. (Voting on demands for grants.)
		5-15 P.M.	His Excellency will preside at the Meeting of the Madras Society for the Protection of Children at 304-a, Tiruvottiyur High Road, Washermanpet.
		6 P.M.	*Her Excellency will preside at the Annual General Meeting of the Red Cross Society in the Banqueting Hall.*
		8-30 P.M.	Dinner and Dance at the Adyar Club.

The four page engagement schedule for the Governor of Madras showing MCC leaving from Central Station, Bombay.

Bodyline would be prepared for Jardine taking time out to accompany his butler to a cemetery in between parties?"

The point is perfectly fair. Guha suggests that India "softened" Jardine and that even if that were not so he was no longer the "cruel and heartless fellow" invoked by so many cricket historians, especially if they come from Australia. That he seemed a different person in the two places is beyond dispute but I don't find that particularly surprising. Australia brought out the worst in him, India bolstered him; and the aspects of his character which felt threatened by Australian cockiness were reassured by the sinuous seductiveness of the Indian establishment. The India he encountered still respected the fancy hat; Australia choked on it.

7

First Test Match, Bombay

Jardine's day out in the company of his family's former butler, now employed by Sir John Beaumont, the Chief Justice, ended tragically. After visiting some of his childhood haunts, Jardine and Lalla Sebastien climbed the hill to the Sewri cemetery and laid their wreaths. Then without warning, the old man began to feel unwell and asked Jardine to walk on ahead and he would catch him up in a few minutes. Jardine assumed the old man wanted a little time alone at his wife's grave so tactfully went on. He waited for a while then returned to find the old man had collapsed.

Jardine rushed him to Bombay's K.E.M. hospital but it was too late. When they arrived there, Lalla Sebastien was pronounced dead.

This strange little tragedy did not interfere with the auspicious game that began on 15 December. Government offices were closed; a new 10,000 capacity double-decker stand was erected and the *Times of India* led with a cartoon of a Lion (England) and a Tiger (India) taking the field under the stiff-lipped caption *"And may the best side win"*. A coin was being tossed by a lion cricketer and a tiger cricketer while a kangaroo in flannels watched from afar. The Gymkhana flew a Union Jack flanked by the 'rhubarb and custard' of MCC on one side and the Indian blue on the other. The so-called Indian flag was that of the English Raj. As that confirmed nationalist Ram Guha puts it, "There was no question of the Bombay Gymkhana putting up in its place the saffron-and-green flag adopted as India's own by the Indian National Congress."

Merchant played again in this first Test though the real hero turned out to be young Lala Amarnath. Merchant made 23 and 30. That fine all-rounder, the Australian Tarrant, also appeared again, this time as one of the umpires. I just wonder if there is any significance in the fact that the two non-Indian umpires gave four of the six top Indian batsmen out lbw in the first innings – they gave none of them in the second. I am also struck by the fact that the Indians scored at only just over two an over in their first innings of 219 while the English managed over three an over in scoring exactly twice as many. The English first innings lead of more than 200 was unassailable. Valentine led the way with 136 which included a six and twelve fours. In support Walters made 78 and Jardine 60. England passed the Indian score with only four wickets down. Five of the Indian team were playing in their first Test match against two Englishmen – Valentine and Arthur Mitchell who opened in both innings and was out for single figures each time.

From an Indian point of view the side's finest hour came too late in the day but it was their finest hour nonetheless. In a single session in the afternoon, the boy Amarnath and his veteran captain C.K. Nayudu put on 186 runs for the third wicket taking the Indians from 21 for two to 207 for three. It was too little, too late but it was still heroic stuff. Amarnath's century was the first ever by an Indian in a Test match. It took three minutes under two hours and included eighteen fours.

The occasion gave rise to a demonstration of the sportsmanship that undoubtedly existed between the two teams. As Amarnath completed his hundred two spectators ran onto the field to celebrate with him. Nayudu, who had just completed the run, left his ground to head off the spectators and to congratulate Amarnath, with the ball still in play. The return came in to the wicket-keeper Elliott who whipped off the bails. Jardine reacted quickly to prevent Elliott from appealing and allowed Nayudu to return to his crease in his own time. Would Jardine have reacted similarly against the Australians?

When Amarnath returned to the pavilion, where he was garlanded by the Mayor, he needed police protection from the masses of spectators that had spilled onto the ground. The *Tribune* reported that at the close of play a part of the crowd "seemed to go mad" breaking chairs and tables in their enthusiasm in front of the Hindu Gymkhana pavilion. Two Maharajahs – Kolhapur and Baroda were among those who congratulated the young hero and local jewellers vied with each other in showering him with gifts. The correspondent of *The Statesman* took a dim view of all this and Amarnath himself said that reports of the largesse were much exaggerated. The *Times of India* correspondent, E.H.D. Sewell remarked sardonically "I hope his head is screwed on firmly". It was.

1933/34 India v England
First Test, Bombay. December 15, 16, 17, 18, 1933
England won by nine wickets.

India
First innings

S Wazir Ali	lbw b Nichols	36
J G Navle	c Nichols b Verity	13
L Amarnath	lbw b Langridge	38
C K Nayudu	lbw b Clark	28
L P Jai	c Mitchell b Langridge	19
V M Merchant	lbw b Nichols	23
S H M Colah	c Elliott b Nichols	31
L Amar Singh	st Elliott b Langridge	0
M Nissar	c Mitchell b Verity	13
L Ramji	b Verity	1
R J D Jamshedji	not out	4
Extras		13
Total (91.2 overs)		219

Fall of wickets	1/44, 2/71, 3/117, 4/135, 5/148, 6/175, 7/186, 8/209, 9/212, 10/219

England Bowling

	O	M	R	W
Nichols	23.2	8	53	3
Clark	13	3	41	1
Barnett	2	1	1	0
Verity	27	11	44	3
Langridge	17	4	42	3
Townsend	9	2	25	0

England
First innings

A Mitchell	b Nissar	5
C F Walters	c Merchant b Amar Singh	78
C J Barnett	c and b Jamshedji	33
J Langridge	lbw b Nissar	31
D R Jardine	b Nissar	60
B H Valentine	c Merchant b Jamshedji	136
L F Townsend	c and b Jamshedji	15
M S Nichols	run out	2
H Verity	c Ramji b Nissar	24
H Elliott	not out	37
E W Clark	b Nissar	1
Extras		16
Total (136.5 overs)		438

Fall of wickets   1/12, 2/67, 3/143, 4/164, 5/309,
6/362, 7/371, 8/373, 9/431, 10/438

India Bowling

	O	M	R	W
Nissar	33.5	3	90	5
Ramji	23	5	64	0
Amar Singh	36	5	119	1
Jamshedji	35	4	137	3
Nayudu	7	2	10	0
Amarnath	2	1	2	0

India
Second innings

S Wazir Ali	c Nichols b Clark	5
J G Navle	c Elliott b Clark	4
L Amarnath	c Nichols b Clark	118
C K Nayudu	c Valentine b Nichols	67
L P Jai	c Jardine b Nichols	0
V M Merchant	c Elliott b Langridge	30
L Amar Singh	lbw b Verity	1
S H M Colah	c Elliott b Nichols	12
M Nissar	lbw b Nichols	1
RJD Jamshedji	not out	1
L Ramji	lbw b Nichols	0
Extras		19
Total (90.5 overs)		258

Fall of wickets   1/9, 2/21, 3/207, 4/208, 5/208,
                      6/214, 7/248, 8/249, 9/258, 10/258

England Bowling

	O	M	R	W
Nichols	23.5	7	55	5
Clark	19	5	69	3
Verity	20	9	50	1
Langridge	16	7	32	1
Townsend	12	5	33	0

England
Second innings

A Mitchell	lbw b Amar Singh	9
C F Walters	not out	14
C J Barnett	not out	17
Extras		0
Total (7.2 overs) (1 wkt)		40

Fall of wickets   1/15

India Bowling

	O	M	R	W
Nissar	4	1	25	0
Amar Singh	3.2	1	15	1

Indian euphoria was all very well but the tourists were able to celebrate Christmas with an unbeaten record which included a comprehensive nine wicket victory in the first Test. It may have been an England second XI but it was, unfortunately perhaps, "fit for purpose". "Toopees off to England" wrote Sewell, adding rather patronisingly, "and hearty congratulations to India on the excellent fight she made of it up to a point." Sewell was a verbose correspondent who seems to have gone largely unsubbed. He was also an author among whose books were *Well Hit Sir!, An Outdoor Wallah* and *Who's Won The Toss?* Jardine himself wrote a letter to the President of the Indian cricket board, an Englishman, paying tribute to "the able and charming captain of the Indian team Major Nayudu". I somehow doubt whether an MCC captain would have paid such a fulsome compliment if the match had been conducted on more equal terms.

8

Second Test Match, Calcutta

The second Test match was scheduled to begin on 5 January, eighteen days after the first one ended. The interval would have been more than adequate but the tourists had four fixtures to fulfil in that time and the little matter of Christmas and New Year to celebrate.

The first match against Poona began on 20 December. It was a two-day affair and resulted in a tame draw. It was largely unmemorable except for some good invididual performances. For MCC, Walters scored 84 of his side's total of 161. Poona in their first innings were skittled out for 83 and Hedley Verity took eight wickets for 37 runs. Nazir Ali scored 57 of Poona's total, a performance which earned him selection for the third Test.

Included in Poona's side was an eighteen-year-old, V.S. Hazare, who would later represent his country in 30 Test matches and score 2,192 runs at a very respectable average of 47.65.

The tourists were in Calcutta for Christmas though the captain was, as so often, away shooting. Jardine wanted a tiger but in Datia, his first stop, he managed only a nilgai and a sambhur. His uncle had once been the Resident in Gwalior so he fancied he might have better luck there. Despite being presented with a matchlock rifle with silver inlaid barrels – a present from the Maharaja – he managed only another sambhur, albeit one with 28 inch horns. He was further incensed when his team-mate "Father" Marriott snaffled a tiger.

The two men missed Christmas with the others and in particular a party on Christmas Eve at which the Mayor of Calcutta made a speech which won Ramachandra Guha's approval by being so dramatically unlike that of the Englishmen. "When the edifice of India's *swaraj* was built historians will take note not only of the contributions made by the politicians but also of those made by sportsmen who would meet their British compeers on an equal ground in the cricket field." I don't get the impression that Jardine and his ilk considered even men such as Nayudu or Amarnath their "compeers". The occasional, massively rich Maharaja, maybe but not a mere cricketer.

There must have been moments on the tour when it seemed that the script had been written by P.G. Wodehouse or A. G. McDonnell. On 27 December, the day after Boxing Day, the tourists turned out for a one-day game against the British in Bengal. It was surprisingly two-sided with MCC making 187 for five declared to which the British in Bengal replied with 121 for eight. "Father" Marriott twirled his leg-spin to devilish effect and took five for 55 including the inevitable Hosie who batted at number three. The British innings was opened by Longfield who was not only a member of the Band of Brothers, a blue, a future big cheese of the Calcutta Club but also the future father-in-law of the patrician England captain, Ted Dexter. His partner Behrend once made 107 for Bengal against the United Provinces and I. P. F. Campbell who went in at four (also a Marriott victim) was a famous soccer player who had once, memorably captained the Sherlock Holmesian actor, Basil Rathbone, while a boy at Repton. Lower down the order Ashfield had turned out for Marlborough College in their big game at Lord's against Rugby and subsequently played for Wiltshire, G.R.R. Brown who came in immediately after him and had M.S. Nichols caught and bowled played occasionally for Essex. One cannot fail to be impressed by the initials, by the sense of grey flannels and Sobranie tobacco, flannelled fools on foreign fields, and a certain sort of forgotten England and Englishman. The world is, of course, a better place without all that, though some die-hards take a different view.

The day after it was the turn of the Indians and Anglo-Indians. This time MCC won by nine wickets though they batted on until they had scored 179 for six, a gesture that pleased the spectators.

The next game, in Calcutta, was played at Eden Gardens against an "Indian XI" though this was something of a misnomer as the Indians were captained by the ubiquitous A.L.Hosie and were almost half composed of Europeans. It seems bizarre, in retrospect that the original itinerary had considered omitting Eden Gardens as a Test match venue for the ground is the oldest in India and dates back to 1864. First class cricket was first played there in 1917-18 and its current capacity is 90,000, a reduction of about 30,000 as the result of modernisation before the World Cup Final in 1987.

The match began on 30 December 1933. MCC batted first and were in trouble at 162 for eight only to be given a little respectability by Townsend and Verity who put on 140 together. Verity scored 91 not out and demonstrated that he was a better batsman than he is usually given credit for. Had he survived the war he might well have developed into an authentic all-rounder.

MCC declared their second innings closed on 279 for five leaving the Indian XI to score 443 for victory This was clearly an impossible task but the "Indians", in the persons mainly of Johnstone and the wicket keeper, Ward, made 152 for the loss of only one wicket. They did so in only 28 overs which suggests that the tourists, who used seven different bowlers were not trying as hard as they might. They, incidentally, scored their 279 second innings' runs in a mere forty five overs. The second innings of both sides sound perilously close to tip-and-run, The MCC rate exceeded six an over and their opponents more than five. The Indian XI included two of the team selected for the second Test match. One was inevitably C.K. Nayudu. The other was M.J. Gopalan who would make his first and only appearance.

1933/34 Indian XI v Marylebone Cricket Club
Eden Gardens, Calcutta. December 30, 31 1933, January 2, 1934
Match drawn.

M. C. C.
First innings

C F Walters	st Ward b Johnstone	67
Mr W H V Levett	c Ward b Gopalan	14
R J Gregory	lbw b Gopalan	8
C J Barnett	lbw b Gopalan	1
M S Nichols	c Longfield b Gopalan	7
Mr D R Jardine	lbw b Longfield	40
Mr B H Valentine	lbw b Longfield	13
Mr J H Human	b Longfield	1
L F Townsend	b Patel	69
H Verity	not out	91
Mr C S Marriott	c Ward b Nayudu	1
Extras		19
Total (125.4 overs)		331

Fall of wickets 1/31, 2/43, 3/49, 4/63, 5/138, 6/148, 7/151, 8/162, 9/302, 10/331

Indian XI Bowling

	O	M	R	W
Longfield	34	10	84	3
Patel	20	3	83	1
Gopalan	34	11	67	4
C K Nayudu	23.4	8	44	1
Johnstone	14	3	34	1

Indian XI
First innings

C P Johnstone	c Jardine b Nichols	6
T C Longfield	lbw b Marriott	22
N M Bose	b Nichols	38
C K Nayudu	c Jardine b Marriott	25
I P F Campbell	lbw b Verity	6
A L Hosie	b Nichols	8
Lall Singh	b Marriott	43
H M Bose	b Nichols	2
H P Ward	b Verity	11
M J Gopalan	run out	0
M S Patel	not out	0
Extras		7
Total (85.1 overs)		168

Fall of wickets   1/21, 2/32, 3/65, 4/74, 5/87, 6/138, 7/143, 8/166, 9/168, 10/168

M. C. C. Bowling

	O	M	R	W
Nichols	19	2	34	4
Valentine	2	0	13	0
Verity	26.1	14	42	2
Marriott	26	12	52	3
Townsend	7	3	11	0
Barnett	2	0	5	0
Human	3	0	4	0

M. C. C.

Second innings

C J Barnett	c Lall Singh b Patel	39
C F Walters	lbw b Patel	12
Mr B H Valentine	c and b Longfield	74
M S Nichols	c Nayudu b Gopalan	79
L F Townsend	b Patel	23
Mr D R Jardine	not out	13
R J Gregory	not out	19
Mr W H V Levett	}	
Mr J H Human	}	
H Verity	} did not bat	
Mr C S Marriott	}	
Extras		20
Total (45 overs) (5 wkts dec)		279

Fall of wickets   1/59, 2/59, 3/160, 4/227, 5/243

Indian XI Bowling

	O	M	R	W
Longfield	15	2	71	1
Patel	11	0	85	3
Gopalan	10	1	32	1
C K Nayudu	6	0	39	0
Johnstone	3	0	32	0

Indian XI
Second innings

C P Johnstone	not out	69
N M Bose	lbw b Valentine	1
H P Ward	not out	77
T C Longfield	}	
C K Nayudu	}	
I P F Campbell	}	
A L Hosie	}	
Lall Singh	} did not bat	
H M Bose	}	
M J Gopalan	}	
M S Patel	}	
Extras		5
Total (28 overs) (1 wkt)		152

Fall of wickets   1/26

M. C. C. Bowling

	O	M	R	W
Nichols	5	0	25	0
Valentine	6	1	19	1
Marriott	3	0	11	0
Barnett	6	0	35	0
Human	3	0	23	0
Walters	2	1	8	0
Gregory	3	0	26	0

The second Test began three days later on the same ground, Eden Gardens. England played an unchanged team with the single exception of wicket-keeper where "Hopper" Levett came in for Elliott. Although the match was drawn it was another essentially one-sided affair. England scored 403 but it took them one delivery short of 160 overs to do it. They then bowled out the home side for

247 and enforced the follow-on. In their second innings the Indians hung on for 237 with the wicket-keeper Dilawar Hussein making his second defiant half century. In all he hit two sixes and fourteen fours. In their final innings the tourists managed only seven for two wickets with Charlie Barnett giving a catch off his very first ball and Valentine falling to a stumping to a clearly elated wicket-keeper. It was his first Test match and as it was also "Hopper" Levett's it seems likely that the duo set an unusual record, the first where both keepers made their debuts.

Jardine was hit in the "abdomen" during the match and the Viceroy turned up as he so often did, accompanied by the Governor of Bengal, Sir John Anderson. Anderson was a Scot who later took to politics and became Home Secretary and Chancellor of the Exchequer in Churchill's wartime government. Immediately before the war he was in charge of air raid precautions and gave his name to the Anderson shelter, a corrugated metal contraption usually erected in people's gardens or public spaces and used as shelters during air raids. It was his most enduring legacy.

The second Test match was played during Ramadan a month in which Muslims traditionally fast. India fielded four Muslims including their fast bowler, Mohammad Nissar, who was presumably feeling peckish since he could only manage four overs before having to be taken off. The *Times of India* was sympathetic and described Nissar's lack of spark as "pardonable", coupling the verdict with some relatively arcane references to armies marching on their stomachs. When the Indians batted Nobby Clark bowled short and hit another Muslim Dilawar Hussein on the head, causing him to leave the field. One of the umpires, the Australian-born mercenary, Frank Tarrant, warned Jardine that if Clark persisted in bowling bumpers he would order him to stop bowling. Jardine, it is said, replied that if he tried any such thing he would prevent Tarrant from umpiring.

1933/34 India v England
Second Test, Calcutta. January 5, 6, 7, 8, 1934
Match drawn.

England
First innings

C F Walters	c Gopalan b Amar Singh	29
A Mitchell	c Gopalan b C K Nayudu	47
C J Barnett	lbw b Amar Singh	8
J Langridge	c Nissar b Gopalan	70
D R Jardine	c C S Nayudu b Mushtaq Ali	61
B H Valentine	lbw b C K Nayudu	40
W H V Levett	b C K Nayudu	5
M S Nichols	lbw b Nissar	13
L F Townsend	c Dilawar Hussein b Amar Singh	40
H Verity	not out	55
E W Clark	c Merchant b Amar Singh	10
Extras		25
Total (159.5 overs)		403

Fall of wickets   1/45, 2/55, 3/135, 4/185, 5/256,
                       6/281, 7/281, 8/301, 9/371, 10/403

India Bowling

	O	M	R	W
Nissar	34	6	112	1
Amar Singh	54.5	13	106	4
Gopalan	19	7	39	1
Mushtaq Ali	19	5	45	1
Amarnath	2	0	10	0
C S Nayudu	8	1	26	0
C K Nayudu	23	7	40	3

India

First innings

Naoomal Jeoomal	c Jardine b Nichols	2
Dilawar Hussain	c Jardine b Clark	59
S Wazir Ali	c Nichols b Verity	39
C K Nayudu	b Clark	5
L Amarnath	c Jardine b Clark	0
V M Merchant	b Verity	54
S Mushtaq Ali	lbw b Nichols	9
C S Nayudu	c Verity b Nichols	36
L Amar Singh	c Nichols b Verity	10
M J Gopalan	not out	11
M Nissar	c Walters b Verity	2
Extras		20
Total (107.4 overs)		247

Fall of wickets   1/12, 2/23, 3/27, 4/90, 5/131,
6/158, 7/211, 8/223, 9/236, 10/247

England Bowling

	O	M	R	W
Clark	26	8	39	3
Nichols	28	6	78	3
Verity	28.4	13	64	4
Langridge	17	7	27	0
Townsend	8	4	19	0

India
Second innings

Naoomal Jeoomal	c Levett b Townsend	43
S Mushtaq Ali	c Barnett b Nichols	18
S Wazir Ali	c Nichols b Verity	0
C K Nayudu	lbw b Verity	38
L Amarnath	c Levett b Clark	9
V M Merchant	c Jardine b Verity	17
Dilawar Hussain	b Clark	57
C S Nayudu	lbw b Verity	15
L Amar Singh	c Jardine b Townsend	18
M J Gopalan	c Levett b Clark	7
M Nissar	not out	0
Extras		15
Total (90.3 overs)		237

Fall of wickets   1/57, 2/58, 3/76, 4/88, 5/129,
6/149, 7/201, 8/214, 9/230,10/237

England Bowling

	O	M	R	W
Clark	19.3	4	50	3
Nichols	20	6	48	1
Verity	31	12	76	4
Langridge	10	4	19	0
Townsend	8	3	22	2
Barnett	2	0	7	0

England
Second innings

C F Walters	not out	2
C J Barnett	c Gopalan b Nissar	0
B H Valentine	st Dilawar Hussain b Nahoomal Jeoomal	3
W H V Levett	not out	2
Extras		0
Total (5 overs) (2 wkts)		7

Fall of wickets   1/0, 2/5

India Bowling

	O	M	R	W
Nissar	2	1	2	1
Amar Singh	2	1	1	0
Nahoomal Jeoomal	1	0	4	1

After the game Willingdon wrote, in a characteristically lofty "survey" that "India will long need the business experience and business gifts of Englishmen." He then departed for an amazing four month period of leave "back home". In his absence the acting viceroy was the Governor of Madras, a time-serving half colonel with the Royal Artillery who just happened to be the sixth son of the 16th Earl of Derby. He almost certainly would not have been where he was if he had not been born with the proverbial silver spoon in his mouth. The medical school in Madras is named after him and he appears to have been precisely the sort of aristocratic type who hastened the demise of the British Empire.

Jardine's apparent truculence did not extend only to Indian cricketers. He had already antagonised the Willingdons but at a ball in the next stop he decided, in the words of Ramachandra Guha, "to misbehave again." This time, he was told at a function held in honour of the Governor of the United Provinces, Sir Malcolm

Hailey, that he was to have the first dance with Lady Hailey. The purveyor of this news was the Military Secretary. Jardine evidently replied "Oh" and waltzed off with the nearest available floosie. When he was taken to task in mid-dance, he apparently "flew into a rage" and said, "I have travelled round the globe but have never been ordered to dance with anybody. I would have danced with Lady Hailey of my own accord, but not if commanded to do so." It was not in Jardine's nature to take orders from anyone, of whatever rank or colour.

Hailey had been Governor of the Punjab for four years before moving to the United Provinces. When he returned to England he was given a peerage and took the title of Baron, linking Shahpur in the Punjab with Newport Pagnell as the two places of which he was Baron. Newport Pagnell was the town of his birth. His only son was killed in the Second World War and when Hailey died in 1969, aged 97, the title died with him. He was a member of the Order of Merit and had a reputation for intellectual brilliance coupled with caution.

Actually Jardine missed out on his choice of dancing partner for Lady Hailey was no ordinary Governor's wife. She was the beautiful and spirited daughter of a Russian Count who, characteristically, walked away from an aeroplane crash in Lahore vowing to take to the air again as soon as possible. She died young, in 1939, and never really adapted to the slightly stuffy ways of the English Raj. Anelterina Balzani would probably have proved more than a match even for Douglas Jardine.

9

First Defeat

After the second Test, the touring party moved on to Benares for the next fixture against the Maharaja Kumar of Vizianagram's XI, played on the Maharaja of Benares' Palace Ground in what is now called Varanasi. A possibly over-confident, even truculent, and well-entertained MCC team suffered their only defeat of the tour.

The umpires yet again were J.W. Hitch and F.A. Tarrant and Vizianagram's team was, apart from himself as captain and number seven batsman, of genuine Test match strength. Also it did not include any Europeans. Instead it boasted C.K. Nayudu himself, S. Wazir Ali and Amarnath as batsmen; the new wicket-keeper Dilawar Hussein and Nissar, the opening bowler who was the real match winner. In their first innings, the home side scored 124 and in reply, the tourists managed a mere 111 runs. Nissar took an impressive six wickets for 60 to give his side a lead on first innings of just thirteen runs which was to prove crucial in Vizzy's eventual fourteen run victory. Vizzy even imported a bowler named Kelaart from what was then Ceylon – another separate pink area, now Sri Lanka of course, and a serious force in international cricket.

It was a low-scoring and closely fought match. In their second innings, the home side scored 140 to set their opponents a target of 154 for victory. A betting man might have been tempted to put his money on MCC at the close of the second day when they were on 59 for 3 with Human and Jardine apparently well set on 16 and 23 respectively. But it was not to be. The following morning Human was bowled by Nissar, as he had been in the first innings, for 18 while Jardine was lbw to Nayudu, his chief adversary, for 36. Nayudu got three lbw decisions in that second innings. A triumphant Vizzy recorded his five hundredth run in first class cricket when, in the first innings, he reached nine out of his final score of 17.

Afterwards it was alleged that Vizzy had induced Jardine to "throw" the match. Ram Guha thinks Vizzy promised Jardine a tiger if MCC lost though others blamed booze or dancing girls. In the event the tiger continued to elude the MCC captain for although he missed the next match shooting in the Maharaja Kumar's personal box in Mirzapur he only managed a bear. Both failures rankled though it appears that the elusive tiger mattered more to Jardine than winning at cricket, or so his detractors believed. I'm not so sure. All the evidence suggests that Jardine absolutely hated losing at cricket, no matter what the game.

1933/34 Maharaja Kumar of Vizianagram's XI v Marylebone Cricket Club

Maharaja of Benares' Palace Ground, Benares. January 10, 11, 12, 1934

Vizianagram's XI won by 14 runs.

Vizianagram's XI
First innings

S Wazir Ali	c Nichols b Clark	12
P E Palia	c Townsend b Nichols	0
L Amarnath	c Valentine b Nichols	4
Major C K Nayudu	c Levett b Townsend	6
The Yuvraj of Patiala	lbw b Townsend	6
Dilawar Hussain	c Jardine b Clark	1
The Maharaja Kumar of Vizianagram	lbw b Townsend	17
E Kelaart	b Townsend	16
C S Nayudu	not out	31
L. Ramji	c Valentine b Townsend	7
Mohammed Nissar	c Levett b Nichols	14
Extras		10
Total (38 overs)		124

Fall of wickets   1/8, 2/14, 3/22, 4/30, 5/31, 6/33, 7/67, 8/72, 9/88, 10/124

M. C. C. Bowling

	O	M	R	W
Clark	12	2	30	2
Nichols	10	0	39	3
Townsend	9	4	30	5
Verity	7	4	15	0

M.C.C.
First innings

Mr C F Walters	b Nissar	13
C J Barnett	c Amarnath b Nissar	4
A H Bakewell	b Ramji	12
Mr J H Human	b Nissar	13
Mr B H Valentine	c Patiala b Ramji	53
M S Nichols	b Nissar	0
Mr D R Jardine	b Nissar	2
L F Townsend	b Nissar	5
H Verity	not out	4
Mr W H V Levett	b Ramji	0
E W Clark	run out	0
Extras		5
Total (41.5 overs)		111

Fall of wickets   1/5, 2/32, 3/35, 468, 5/70, 6/79,
7/107, 8/107, 9/111, 10/111

Vizianagram's XI Bowling

	O	M	R	W
Nissar	20	4	60	6
Ramji	19.5	4	42	3
C K Nayudu	1	0	2	0
Kelaart	1	0	2	0

Vizianagram's XI
Second innings

Dilawar Hussain	c and b Nichols	18
S Wazir Ali	c Bakewell b Clark	5
L Amarnath	c Levett b Verity	22
Major C K Nayudu	c Bakewell b Verity	17
The Yuvraj of Patiala	b Nichols	44
P E Palia	c Levett b Clark	14
The Maharaja Kumar of Vizianagram	c Valentine b Clark	2
E Kelaart	b Nichols	6
C S Nayudu	c Human b Verity	5
L Ramji	b Verity	4
Mohammed Nissar	not out	0
Extras		3
Total (41.2 overs)		140

Fall of wickets   1/19, 2/28, 3/57, 4/64, 5/91, 6/101, 7/128, 8/135, 9/140, 10/140

M. C. C. Bowling

	O	M	R	W
Clark	13	2	32	3
Nichols	7.2	0	48	3
Townsend	7	1	18	0
Verity	14	4	39	4

M.C.C.
Second innings

Mr C F Walters	lbw b Ramji	2
A H Bakewell	c Amarnath b Ramji	15
C J Barnett	c Patiala b Ramji	4
Mr J H Human	b Nissar	18
Mr D R Jardine	lbw b C K Nayudu	36
Mr B H Valentine	c Palia b Nissar	4
H Verity	lbw b C K Nayudu	18
M S Nichols	lbw b C K Nayudu	0
L F Townsend	c Wazir Ali b Nissar	34
Mr W H V Levett	b C K Nayudu	1
E W Clark	not out	4
Extras		3
Total (65.3 overs)		139

Fall of wickets 1/2, 2/10, 3/23, 4/62, 5/66, 6/94, 7/94, 8/133, 9/134, 10/139

Vizianagram's XI Bowling

	O	M	R	W
Nissar	23	8	57	3
Ramji	21	8	39	3
C K Nayudu	8.3	2	24	4
Kelaart	13	7	16	0

In the tourists' next match against Central Provinces and Berar, C.K. Nayudu made a century for the hosts but the next highest score was only 27 and his side were all out for 195 with Marriott taking six for 35. This game was played at the Vidarbha Cricket Association Ground in Nagpur. Nagpur is located in the centre of India and is one of the main areas where oranges are grown. Otherwise it's a nondescript place and noteworthy only for the annual Dussehra Festival which is held in September or October.

Nayudu followed up his century by bowling 29 overs and taking five wickets for 87 but the tourists still managed to gain a useful, if not overwhelming, first innings lead of 66. In their second innings the home side lost four wickets for just 35 and although they rallied to reach 188 it was not enough to prevent the MCC achieving a comfortable six wicket victory. The batsmen out, Gregory, Barnett, Mitchell and Jardine were all adjudged leg before wicket. Five members of the home team were making their debuts in first-class cricket.

1933/34 Central Provinces and Berar v Marylebone Cricket Club
Vidarbha Cricket Association Ground, Nagpur. January 19, 20, 21, 1934
MCC won by six wickets.

Central Provinces and Berar
First innings

S K Razak	c and b Human	12
Rahman Pasha	b Marriott	27
D R Rutnam	c Mitchell b Verity	15
Major C K Nayudu	st Levett b Marriott	107
C S Nayudu	lbw b Marriott	21
G R Nayudu	b Marriott	4
R K Rao	c Nichols b Human	0
T S Nayudu	b Marriott	0
C L Nayudu	c Verity b Marriott	0
S H Razak	c Jardine b Verity	2
Tatarao	not out	0
Extras		7
Total (70.3 overs)		195

Fall of wickets   1/41, 2/41, 3/82, 4/146, 5/168,
                         6/173, 7/182, 8/192, 9/195, 10/195

M. C. C. Bowling

	O	M	R	W
Clark	11	0	28	0
Nichols	11	0	44	0
Verity	14.3	3	36	2
Marriott	23	11	35	6
Human	11	1	45	2

M. C. C.
First innings

C J Barnett	c Rahman Pasha b Tatarao	140
Mr W H V Levett	b Tatarao	20
A Mitchell	lbw b C K Nayudu	6
R J Gregory	b G R Nayudu	13
Mr D R Jardine	b Tatarao	27
Mr B H Valentine	lbw b C K Nayudu	1
M S Nichols	c S H Razak b C K Nayudu	5
Mr J H Human	b C K Nayudu	5
H Verity	lbw b Tatarao	13
Mr C S Marriott	b C K Nayudu	5
E W Clark	not out	3
Extras		23
Total (86 overs)		261

Fall of wickets   1/51, 2/60, 3/88, 4/157, 5/162,
                         6/182, 7/192, 8/231, 9/252, 10/261

Central Provinces and Berar Bowling

	O	M	R	W
C S Nayudu	12	1	40	0
C K Nayudu	29.1	6	87	5
G R Nayudu	11	4	30	1
Rahman Pasha	4	0	21	0
R K Rao	2	1	4	0
Tartarao	28	9	56	4

Central Provinces and Berar

Second innings

S K Razak	c Jardine b Verity	11
Rahman Pasha	c Gregory b Mitchell	7
D R Rutnam	c Levett b Nichols	21
S H Razak	c Human b Verity	10
R K Rao	c Mitchell b Marriott	0
T S Nayudu	b Nichols	32
Major C K Nayudu	c Jardine b Human	8
C S Nayudu	not out	61
C L Nayudu	c Gregory b Verity	7
G R Nayudu	run out	0
Tatarao	st Levett b Human	4
Extras		7
Total (79.4 overs)		188

Fall of wickets   1/12, 2/22, 3/32, 4/35, 5/76, 6/92, 7/128, 8/181, 9/181, 10/188

M. C. C. Bowling

	O	M	R	W
Clark	16	7	34	0
Nichols	6	0	18	2
Verity	14	5	35	3
Marriott	16	5	50	1
Human	4.3	0	34	2
Mitchell	4	1	10	1

M. C. C.
Second innings

R J Gregory	lbw b Tatarao	5
C J Barnett	lbw b C K Nayudu	35
A Mitchell	lbw b C S Nayudu	9
Mr B H Valentine	not out	50
Mr D R Jardine	lbw b C K Nayudu	18
M S Nichols	not out	12
Mr W H V Levett }		
Mr J H Human }		
H Verity }	did not bat	
Mr C S Marriott }		
E W Clark }		
Extras		0
Total (31 overs) (4 wkts)		129

Fall of wickets   1/9, 2/33, 3/74, 4/112

Central Provinces and Berar Bowling

	O	M	R	W
C S Nayudu	8	0	30	1
C K Nayudu	12	1	44	2
G R Nayudu	4	1	27	0
Tartarao	7	0	28	1

Although he did not play in the match, a somewhat disgruntled Jardine did go to a reception for his team where he apparently railed against the aspiring leaders of India, saying that if they raised a cricket team they would "question the umpire's decision". That was clearly something Jardine would never have done although he might have tried to tell the umpire what the decision should be.

Hitch and Tarrant were umpiring again when MCC moved on to the Gymkhana Ground at Secunderabad where they drew their match against the Nawab of Moin-ud-Dowlah's team, though the Nawab himself did not actually play. Secunderabad is actually the more drab and less visited twin of the more exotic and better known Hyderabad, City of Pearls and the most significant Muslim centre in India. The two cities are usually lumped together and known as Hyderabad. Cricket had been introduced to the Hyderabad area in the 1880s by the British Army but although an Oxford Authentics team had visited the city at the turn of the century there was no first-class cricket there until 1930. That was when the Nawab, a keen patron of the game, instituted a Gold Cup and the English stars, Hobbs and Sutcliffe were imported to play.

1933/34 Nawab of Moin-ud-Dowlah's XI v Marylebone Cricket Club
Gymkhana Ground, Secunderabad. January 23, 24, 25, 1934
Match drawn.

M.C.C.
First innings

Mr C F Walters	b Mushtaq Ali	18
A Mitchell	c Hadi b Mushtaq Ali	10
A H Bakewell	lbw b Mushtaq Ali	2
H Verity	lbw b C K Nayudu	19
Mr B H Valentine	lbw b Mushtaq Ali	10
J Langridge	not out	13
R J Gregory	lbw b Amar Singh	7
L F Townsend	c Hussein b Mushtaq Ali	12
M S Nichols	c Amarnath b Amar Singh	15
Mr J H Human	lbw b Amar Singh	1
Mr W H V Levett	lbw b Amar Singh	0
Extras		5
Total (49.1 overs)		112

Fall of wickets   1/31, 2/32, 3/39, 4/57, 5/63, 6/73, 7/90, 8/110, 9/112, 10/112

Moin-ud-Dowlah's XI Bowling

	O	M	R	W
Amar Singh	13.1	1	33	4
Nazir Ali	3	1	8	0
Mushtaq Ali	15	6	37	5
Bharat Chand	3	2	1	0
C K Nayudu	14	0	24	1
C S Nayudu	1	0	4	0

Moin-ud-Dowlah's XI
First innings

Naoomal Jeoomal	c Human b Mitchell	11
Mushtaq Ali	b Verity	27
L Amarnath	c Walters b Townsend	7
Major C K Nayudu	c Walters b Townsend	2
C S Nayudu	b Verity	0
S M Hussein	lbw b Langridge	7
Nazir Ali	c Bakewell b Verity	43
Amar Singh	c Gregory b Townsend	58
S M Hadi	b Verity	23
Bharat Chand	b Verity	8
Vajubha	not out	2
Extras		6
Total (55 overs)		194

Fall of wickets   1/15, 2/39, 3/49, 4/49, 5/49, 6/75,
7/127, 8/173, 9/184, 10/194

M. C. C. Bowling

	O	M	R	W
Nichols	5	1	15	0
Mitchell	2	0	10	1
Townsend	19	5	65	3
Langridge	7	1	35	1
Verity	22	10	63	5

M. C. C.
Second innings

Mr C F Walters	c Hussain b Mushtaq Ali	36
A Mitchell	lbw b Amarnath	42
J Langridge	c C S Nayudu b Amarnath	29
Mr B H Valentine	b Amar Singh	29
A H Bakewell	c Mushtaq Ali b Amar Singh	18
R J Gregory	lbw b Amar Singh	33
L F Townsend	c Hussein b Amarnath	21
M S Nichols	not out	55
H Verity	lbw b Amar Singh	8
Mr J H Human	c and b Amar Singh	4
Mr W H V Levett	lbw b C K Nayudu	9
Extras		19
Total (118.3 overs)		303

Fall of wickets   1/71, 2/117, 3/118, 4/133, 5/168,
                         6/203, 7/221, 8/260, 9/264, 10/303

Moin-ud-Dowlah's XI Bowling

	O	M	R	W
Amar Singh	42	9	82	5
Nazir Ali	12	2	32	0
Mushtaq Ali	18	3	46	1
Bharat Chand	2	1	2	0
C K Nayudu	12.3	4	20	1
C S Nayudu	5	1	17	0
Naoomal Jeoomal	1	0	1	0
Amarnath	26	5	84	3

Moin-ud-Dowlah's XI
Second innings

Naoomal Jeoomal	lbw b Verity	16
Mushtaq Ali	st Levett b Townsend	26
L Amarnath	c Nichols b Townsend	0
Major C K Nayudu	c Mitchell b Nichols	79
C S Nayudu	c Langridge b Verity	25
S M Hussein	c Gregory b Townsend	21
Amar Singh	c Mitchell b Verity	0
Nazir Ali	c Langridge b Townsend	3
S M Hadi	not out	4
Bharat Chand	c Mitchell b Human	1
Vajubha	not out	8
Extras		5
Total (61 overs) (9 wkts)		188

Fall of wickets   1/31, 2/38, 3/49, 4/127, 5/129,
6/141, 7/172, 8/176, 9/179

M. C. C. Bowling

	O	M	R	W
Nichols	6	1	16	1
Townsend	24	3	76	4
Langridge	1	0	5	0
Verity	29	9	78	3
Human	1	0	8	1

The tourists, captained by Walters in the absence of Jardine, only managed 112 in their first innings and no-one even made as many as 20. The home side were almost as bad until a late rally which resulted in over a hundred runs for the last four wickets and a lead of 82. MCC performed better in their second innings and their total of 303 left the hosts needing 222 runs for victory. Although C.K.

Nayudu made 79 in the Nawab's second innings the match closed with the home side on 188 for nine, still 34 runs short of their target.

Back in England the number of questionable lbw decisions was a matter of concern and Hitch and Tarrant were not above suspicion. After all, in the match against the Nawab of Moin-ud-Dowlah's team they had given no less than six of the tourists out leg before wicket in that disastrous first innings. When it was the Indians' turn to bat Hitch and Tarrant only allowed one lbw appeal and the home side led by a healthy 82 runs. In the second innings four of the tourists were given out leg before while in the Nawab's second innings the umpires again allowed only one. It was reported in *The Times* that after the match no less a person than Sir Stanley Jackson, presiding over the annual general meeting of the Yorkshire County Cricket Club "expressed keen regret at the inordinate number of decisions for lbw given against the English batsmen at present touring in India". Sir Stanley was, of course, thousands of miles away whereas Hitch and Tarrant were standing at the bowler's end. Nevertheless there is no doubt that statistically Sir Stanley had a point. England was watching.

10

Third Test Match, Madras

Jardine was back to captain the side against Madras at the city's MA Chidambaram Stadium on 3 February and although he made only 37 himself the team amassed 603 with Mitchell making 161 and Bakewell 158. C.P. Johnstone, who passed 3,500 first-class runs in the second innings was the Madras hired hand but although he made 46 in the first innings and 69 in the second, top-scoring on both occasions, his efforts were not enough to prevent Madras succumbing to an embarrassing defeat by an innings and 352 runs. Marriott got a hat trick in the Madras second innings.

The third and final Test match took place on the same ground and England were unchanged except that Elliott regained his place from Hopper Levett and kept wicket. Bakewell came in for Valentine and made top score in the first innings with 85. Amar Singh took seven for 86 but the tourists still made 335 in reply to which India could only manage 145 with Verity taking seven for 49, his best Test match bowling figures thus far. This was enough. England did not enforce the follow-on and batted a second time with Walters scoring 102. This was his first Test century, his previous highest score having been 78. Jardine declared on 261 for seven. In their final innings India made 249 with Verity and Langridge sharing the nine wickets - Naoomal Jeoomal retired hurt after scoring five in the first innings and took no further part in the game. The Indian total was 202 runs short.

1933/34 India v England
Third Test, Madras. February 10, 11, 12, 13, 1934
England won by 202 runs.

England
First innings

A H Bakewell	c C S Nayudu b Amarnath	85
C F Walters	lbw b Amar Singh	59
A Mitchell	lbw b Amarnath	25
J Langridge	lbw b Amar Singh	1
D R Jardine	c Wazir Ali b Amar Singh	65
C J Barnett	c Patiala b Amar Singh	4
M S Nichols	b Amar Singh	1
L F Townsend	b Amar Singh	10
H Verity	lbw b Mushtaq Ali	42
H Elliott	c Mushtaq Ali b Amar Singh	14
E W Clark	not out	4
Extras		25
Total (131.4 overs)		335

Fall of wickets   1/111, 2/167, 3/170, 4/174, 5/178,
6/182, 7/208, 8/305, 9/317, 10/335

India Bowling

	O	M	R	W
Amar Singh	44.4	13	86	7
C K Nayudu	11	1	32	0
Amarnath	31	14	69	2
Mushtaq Ali	25	3	64	1
C S Nayudu	13	1	43	0
Naoomal Jeoomal	6	0	16	0
Wazir Ali	1	1	0	0

India
First innings

Dilawar Hussain	c Barnett b Verity	13
Naoomal Jeoomal	retired hurt	5
S Wazir Ali	b Nichols	2
C K Nayudu	b Verity	20
L Amarnath	c Elliott b Langridge	12
V M Merchant	b Verity	26
Yuvraj of Patiala	b Verity	24
S Nazir Ali	c Mitchell b Verity	3
C S Nayudu	c Nichols b Verity	11
S Mushtaq Ali	not out	7
L Amar Singh	c Barnett b Verity	16
Extras		6
Total (59.5 overs)		145

Fall of wickets 1/15, 2/39, 3/42, 4/66, 5/99, 6/107, 7/122, 8/127, 9/145

England Bowling

	O	M	R	W
Clark	15	4	37	0
Nichols	12	3	30	1
Verity	23.5	10	49	7
Langridge	6	1	9	1
Townsend	3	0	14	0

England
Second innings

A H Bakewell	c Patiala b Amar Singh	4
C F Walters	c sub b Amarnath	102
C J Barnett	c Mushtaq Ali b Nazir Ali	26
L F Townsend	c C K Nayudu b Nazir Ali	8
M S Nichols	c Dilawar Hussein b Nazir Ali	8
J Langridge	c Dilawar Hussein b Nazir Ali	46
D R Jardine	not out	35
A Mitchell	c and b Amarnath	28
H Verity	}	
H Elliott	} did not bat	
E W Clark	}	
Extras		4
Total (75.5 overs) (7 wkts dec.)		261

Fall of wickets   1/10, 2/76, 3/90, 4/102, 5/184,
                         6/209, 7/261

India Bowling

	O	M	R	W
Amar Singh	23	6	55	1
Nazir Ali	23	1	83	4
C K Nayudu	9	0	38	0
Amarnath	11.5	3	32	2
Mushtaq Ali	4	0	16	0
C S Nayudu	2	0	17	0
Wazir Ali	3	0	16	0

India

Second innings

Dilawar Hussain	b Langridge	36
S Mushtaq Ali	c Mitchell b Verity	8
S Wazir Ali	c Mitchell b Verity	21
L Amar Singh	c Barnett b Langridge	48
C K Nayudu	st Elliott b Langridge	2
V M Merchant	c and b Verity	28
Yuvraj of Patiala	c Elliott b Langridge	60
L Amarnath	not out	26
S Nazir Ali	c Nichols b Langridge	8
C S Nayudu	st Elliott b Verity	0
Naoomal Jeoomal	absent hurt	0
Extras		12
Total (69.2 overs)		249

Fall of wickets   1/16, 2/45, 3/119, 4/120, 5/125,
6/209, 7/237, 8/248, 9/249

England Bowling

	O	M	R	W
Clark	8	2	27	0
Nichols	6	1	23	0
Verity	27.2	6	104	4
Langridge	24	5	63	5
Barnett	1	0	1	0
Townsend	3	0	19	0

Tarrant was to have been an umpire in this game but was stood down at the last moment at Jardine's insistence. There is some speculation about whether or not this was related to the contretemps over Nobby Clark's bouncers in Calcutta or because Tarrant's favourite pupil, Patiala's son, the Yuvraj, had been chosen to play for India. Guha takes Tarrant's side, describing him as "a great servant of Indian cricket and a mentor to many of its players". The Indians stayed away from a dinner after the match given by the "all-white" Madras Cricket Club and Guha wonders if this was a protest against Jardine's "admittedly brief resort to Bodyline" (he had encouraged Clark to bowl more lethal bouncers in Tarrant's absence), or to "a general disgust with the ways of the English in India".

Tarrant gave an interview to the *Times of India* in which he claimed that Jardine hadn't liked some of the decisions he had given earlier. "Where are the sportsmen of 1934 if the captain of the MCC cannot take lbw decisions with good grace?", Guha quotes the *Sind Observer* which alleged that Tarrant's suspension was "symptomatic of the spirit in which Mr. Jardine conducts his captaincy". According to the paper he "seems to feel that he is an Imperial General on a conquering expedition".

This is quite possibly a fair description of the Jardine captaincy but Tarrant sounds suspiciously one-eyed as well. It would have been more sensible for Jardine to have protested at Tarrant's appointment as umpire, fine cricketer though he almost certainly was. Expecting Jardine to take his lbw decisions with "good grace" is either naïve or mendacious.

For the final match of the tour MCC returned to Bombay for a fixture against an Indian XI. The match was not part of the original schedule but was a last-minute addition played for the benefit of the Indian Earthquake Fund. There had been an earthquake in Bihar and a special "Viceroy's Fund" had been created to assist the victims. Paternalist, possibly, but the Raj, it seems, was often generous provided its real interests were not threatened and the rulers could go on ruling. Acts of generosity didn't excuse the regime but showed its human side.

The formidable C.K. Nayudu was unavailable for the Indian XI so they were captained by the Maharaja Kumar of Vizianagram, whose own team had inflicted the only defeat of the tour so far on Jardine's men. It was a close game. The tourists scored 224 in their first innings to which the opener Mitchell contributed 91. The Indian XI replied with 238 to lead MCC by 14 on first innings. In their second innings MCC were all out for 215 so the Indians required 202 to win. Vizzy's team had a lengthy tail including Vizzy himself so were vulnerable. Hedley Verity had yet to take a wicket in the match so was surely due for some. It was still anybody's game.

In the end Vizzy's men batted so slowly that they lost any chance of victory. At the close they were on 112 for four wickets after 61 overs. Jamshedji who was number 11 in the first innings was promoted to number 4 and spent two and a half hours in scoring 17 runs. Vijay Merchant had made 89 not out in the first innings and was 18 not out at the close. With more time he might have made a game of it but it was not to be and the match ended in a draw.

The game was played at the Bombay Gymkhana and the secretary, a man named Prideaux, seems to have behaved with oafish jobsworthiness by allocating free passes only to the *Associated Press* and the *Times of India*. A dozen Indian journalists were told to buy tickets if they wanted to watch the game but their masters retaliated by refusing to report the match at all – earthquake or no earthquake.

1933/34 An Indian XI v Marylebone Cricket Club
Gymkhana Ground, Bombay. March 4, 5, 6, 1934
Match drawn.

M. C. C.
First innings

A Mitchell	b Amarnath	91
A H Bakewell	c Amar Singh b Richards	0
R J Gregory	lbw b Amar Singh	18
C J Barnett	lbw b Amarnath	0
Mr D R Jardine	lbw b Amarnath	15
Mr B H Valentine	b Richards	38
H Verity	b Amar Singh	4
L F Townsend	c Amarnath b C S Nayudu	21
M S Nichols	c Dilawar Hussain b Amar Singh	20
Mr W H V Levett	run out	9
Mr C S Marriott	not out	3
Extras		5
Total (72.2 overs)		224

Fall of wickets   1/4, 2/37, 3/38, 4/58, 5/136, 6/145,
7/182, 8/202, 9/215, 10/224

Indian XI Bowling

	O	M	R	W
Amar Singh	32.2	8	75	3
Richards	11	1	53	2
Amarnath	20	5	43	3
Vajifdar	4	0	11	0
Jamshedji	3	0	16	0
C S Nayudu	2	0	21	1

An Indian XI
First innings

S Wazir Ali	b Barnett	27
Dilawar Hussein	c Levett b Barnett	35
C Mehta	c Mitchell b Townsend	36
V M Merchant	not out	89
L Amarnath	c Levett b Nichols	11
H J Vajifdar	b Nichols	0
The Maharaja Kumar of Vizianagram	b Nichols	4
Amar Singh	b Marriott	1
G Richards	c Barnett b Marriott	0
C S Nayudu	st Levett b Townsend	17
R J Jamshedji	b Nichols	0
Extras		18
Total (73.5 overs)		238

Fall of wickets   1/64, 2/65, 3/140, 4/157, 5/157,
                         6/168, 7/178, 8/178, 9/220, 10/238

M. C. C. Bowling

	O	M	R	W
Nichols	21.5	3	68	4
Marriott	20	5	58	2
Verity	19	5	58	0
Barnett	6	1	26	2
Townsend	7	2	10	2

M. C. C.

Second innings

A Mitchell	lbw b Amar Singh	20
A H Bakewell	b Amar Singh	56
C J Barnett	c Dilawar Hussain b Amar Singh	13
R J Gregory	b Amarnath	6
Mr D R Jardine	c sub b C S Nayudu	26
Mr B H Valentine	b Richards	21
H Verity	lbw b Richards	11
L F Townsend	lbw b Amar Singh	16
M S Nichols	c Richards b Amar Singh	28
Mr W H V Levett	not out	8
Mr C S Marriott	b Amarnath	5
Extras		5
Total (73.3 overs)		215

Fall of wickets   1/26, 2/42, 3/49, 4/105, 5/139,
6/149, 7/157, 8/189, 9/210, 10/215

Indian XI Bowling

	O	M	R	W
Amar Singh	32	6	109	5
Richards	16	4	51	2
Amarnath	15.3	5	23	2
Vajifdar	4	0	9	0
C S Nayudu	5	0	14	1
Merchant	1	0	4	0

An Indian XI
Second innings

S Wazir Ali	lbw b Marriott	28
Dilawar Hussein	c Barnett b Nichols	0
L Amarnath	st Levett b Marriott	29
R J Jamshedji	b Nichols	17
V M Merchant	not out	18
C Mehta	not out	10
H J Vajifdar		
The Maharaja Kumar }		
of Vizianagram }		
Amar Singh }	did not bat	
G Richards }		
C S Nayudu }		
Extras		10
Total (61 overs) (4 wkts)		112

Fall of wickets   1/1, 2/38, 3/82, 4/88

M. C. C. Bowling

	O	M	R	W
Nichols	16	6	20	2
Marriott	15	7	25	2
Verity	9	2	26	0
Barnett	4	4	0	0
Townsend	15	6	23	0
Jardine	1	0	1	0
Mitchell	1	0	7	0

11

Aftermath

When the tourists had packed up and moved on, the *Times of India* opined that it had all gone wonderfully well and laid the foundations of another great straight-batted games playing nation within the British Commonwealth. Not everyone agreed and our old friend Mr. Guha reported the *Bombay Chronicle*'s verdict that the visit had been marred by "a series of inexcusable and egregious blunders and bunglings. The composition of the Selection Committee, with a majority of non-Indians, the appointment of umpires (no Indian was on the panel) and the unfortunate episode in Madras – all these have brought into prominent relief the utter failure of the Board of Control for Cricket in India to maintain the self-respect of Indians."

On 29 March 1934, ten of the team together with their manager, Major Ricketts, arrived in Plymouth aboard the R.M.S. *Rawalpindi*. The ship was a P & O liner, but newer and smaller than the *Mooltan*. Like her sister "R" class ships her interiors had been designed by the daughter of the shipping magnate Lord Inchcape. The *Rawalpindi* was later requisitioned by the Admiralty, turned into an armed merchantman and sunk by the German ships, *Scharnhorst* and *Gneisenau* off the coast of Iceland.

Jardine himself remained in India, predictably enough for some more shooting. He had already informed his county, Surrey, that he would no longer be able to play regularly for them, a decision which was greeted with "great regret", though one can't help feeling that the private and more honest reaction was some relief.

H.D.G. Leveson Gower, later Sir Henry, but nicknamed "Shrimp", Surrey's president, announced that E.R.T. (Errol) Holmes, an altogether easier and more genial fellow, would take over. Holmes continued to play for Surrey into the 1950s and was always a more popular and flexible captain. His batting average however was ten less than Jardine's and he lacked his predecessor's implacable obduracy.

Back in Plymouth Major Ricketts said that the tour had been "strenuous but very successful." The Major thought that during the past two or three years cricket in India had shown "vast improvements". He was not, one cannot help feeling, a Major for nothing.

Years later, in 1958, Jardine died of cancer in a Swiss clinic. He was only 57 years of age. He had been rejected by the British Establishment and utterly eclipsed by his old enemy, Bradman. Retirement and ostracism seemed to have mellowed him and he had even developed an interest in Hinduism allied to a hostility to orthodox Christianity. Towards the end of his life he was no more orthodox than he had been in the days of his youth, though he was, arguably a nicer, more tolerant person.

In an obituary in a Madras weekly his old adversary Major Nayudu saluted him in the measured, respectful tones which became usual when considering him. Nayudu paid tribute to his tough fighting qualities, his sound even profound knowledge of cricket, his imposing physical presence. Nayudu concluded "He was a strict disciplinarian and would not tolerate any opposition. He was aloof and unsentimental. He commanded loyalty rather than won it."

All this is true, no doubt. On the other hand I think of all those mildly absurd Indian princes, the ghastly Willingdons, the frequent and often frustrating tiger hunts, the flashes of temper, glimpses of humour and perhaps above all the loyalty he inspired in those he led and the treachery in those he sought to represent. I think, naturally, of the Bodyline tour of Australia for which he is so often remembered but I think too of the strange aftermath in India which is so often neglected. He was a lonely, driven little boy at preparatory school in England and he died prematurely in a foreign country, intrigued by the exotic foreign religion he had first encountered in the country of his birth.

I shall remember him for his Indian adventures and think of him as likeable in an odd way, lonely, human, unconventional but, above all, complicated.

Appendix I

Marylebone Cricket Club.
Tour of India and Ceylon, 1933/34
Details of other first class matches

1933/34 Madras v Marylebone Cricket Club
M A Chidambaram Stadium, Chepauk, Madras. February 3, 4, 5, 1934
M. C. C. won by an innings and 352 runs.

M. C. C.
First innings

C J Barnett	c Johnstone b Gopalan	4
A H Bakewell	c Johnstone b Gopalan	158
R J Gregory	b Palia	66
A Mitchell	c Hussain b Johnstone	161
Mr B H Valentine	b Palia	44
Mr D R Jardine	c Gopalan b Palia	37
J Langridge	lbw b Gopalan	4
L F Townsend	not out	53
H Elliott	b Palia	29
E W Clark	b Bharat Chand	11
Mr C S Marriott	lbw b Bharat Chand	0
Extras		36
Total (161 overs)		603

Fall of wickets   1/18, 2/179, 3/258, 4/336, 5/441,
6/456, 7/509, 8/564, 9/603, 10/603

Madras Bowling

	O	M	R	W
Gopalan	37	6	113	3
Bharat Chand	29	6	106	2
Ramsingh	17	4	33	0
McIntosh	17	1	74	0
Johnstone	24	2	103	1
Palia	34	2	117	4
Nailer	2	0	10	0
Uttappa	1	0	11	0

Madras
First innings

C P Johnstone	b Townsend	46
Bharat Chand	c Jardine b Townsend	18
H P Ward	b Townsend	0
P E Palia	c Gregory b Marriott	0
S M Hussain	lbw b Marriott	21
Captain F G Rogers	b Langridge	5
A C Ramsingh	b Clark	0
R Nailer	b Clark	0
M A Uttappa	b Clark	1
M Gopalan	c Elliott b Marriott	12
R I F McIntosh	not out	0
Extras		3
Total (42.5 overs)		106

Fall of wickets   1/61, 2/65, 3/70, 4/71, 5/88, 6/90, 7/90, 8/92, 9/106, 10/106

M. C. C. Bowling

	O	M	R	W
Clark	9	2	15	3
Barnett	2	0	13	0
Marriott	14.5	6	5	3
Townsend	14	3	36	3
Langridge	3	2	4	1

Madras
Second innings

C P Johnstone	c and b Townsend	69
Bharat Chand	b Clark	1
S M Hussain	lbw b Marriott	5
H P Ward	b Clark	12
Captain F G Rogers	c Townsend b Langridge	10
M Gopalan	c Gregory b Marriott	6
A C Ramsingh	st Elliott b Marriott	2
R Nailer	b Marriott	0
M A Uttappa	b Marriott	0
P E Palia	not out	18
R I F McIntosh	run out	1
Extras		21
Total (72.2 overs)		145

Fall of wickets   1/26, 2/40, 3/70, 4/91, 5/100,6/120, 7/120, 8/120, 9/126, 10/145

M. C. C. Bowling

	O	M	R	W
Clark	16	6	24	2
Barnett	2	1	1	0
Marriott	22	6	43	5
Townsend	21	7	34	1
Langridge	11.2	4	22	1

1933/34 All Ceylon XI v Marylebone Cricket Club
Colombo. February 16, 17, 18, 1934
MCC won by ten wickets

All Ceylon XI
First innings

M K Albert	c Barnet b Clark	3
W T Brindley	lbw b Nichols	17
F A Waldock	b Nichols	0
L D S Gunasekara	c Levett b Clark	3
S S Jayawickreme	c Gregory b Nichols	15
N S Joseph	b Clark	19
D B Gunasekara	b Nichols	4
V C Schockman	not out	22
Dr C H Gunasekara	c Jardine b Clark	14
B de Kretser	c Langridge b Clark	0
D S Jayasundera	c Townsend b Clark	8
Extras		1
Total (40 overs)		106

Fall of wickets   1/6, 2/7, 3/10, 4/39, 5/40, 6/46,
7/64, 8/86, 9/96, 10/106

M. C. C. Bowling

	O	M	R	W
Clark	9	1	24	6
Nichols	9	1	29	4
Marriott	13	3	35	0
Langridge	9	4	17	0

M. C. C.
First innings

A H Bakewell	c Jayasundera b de Kretser	48
Mr W H V Levett	lbw b Brindley	14
R J Gregory	b D B Gunasekera	2
J Langridge	c Schokman b Jayawickreme	44
C J Barnett	lbw b Brindley	116
Mr D R Jardine	c Jayasundera b Joseph	4
Mr J H Human	lbw b D B Gunasekera	15
M S Nichols	c D B Gunasekera b Brindley	8
L F Townsend	not out	9
E W Clark	c Jayasundera b Brindley	4
Mr C S Marriott	c C H Gunasekera b Brindley	0
Extras		8
Total (80.4 overs)		272

Fall of wickets   1/47, 2/65, 3/67, 4/203, 5/208, 6/243, 7/259, 8/260, 9/268, 10/272

All Ceylon XI Bowling

	O	M	R	W
de Kretser	23	1	51	1
Brindley	15.4	3	40	5
D B Gunasekara	11	1	51	2
Jayawickreme	8	1	40	1
Joseph	5	0	24	1
C H Gunasekara	4	1	16	0
D S Jayasundera	14	3	42	0

All Ceylon XI
Second innings

M K Albert	c Levett b Nichols	16
W T Brindley	c Nichols b Clark	2
F A Waldock	lbw b Human	29
L D S Gunasekara	c Jardine b Clark	4
S S Jayawickreme	b Human	21
N S Joseph	c Marriott b Clark	78
D B Gunasekara	b Langridge	11
V C Schockman	b Langridge	0
Dr C H Gunasekara	c Jardine b Clark	17
B de Kretser	not out	2
D S Jayasundera	st Levette b Marriott	5
Extras		4
Total (43 overs)		189

Fall of wickets   1/20, 2/26, 3/26, 4/71, 5/78, 6/106, 7/106, 8/165, 9/183, 10/189

M. C. C. Bowling

	O	M	R	W
Clark	13	1	49	4
Nichols	8	0	47	1
Marriott	10	3	28	1
Langridge	7	1	40	2
Human	5	0	21	2

M. C. C.
Second innings

A H Bakewell	not out	13
Mr W H V Levett	not out	12
R J Gregory	}	
J Langridge	}	
C J Barnett	}	
Mr D R Jardine	}	
Mr J H Human	} did not bat	
M S Nichols	}	
L F Townsend	}	
E W Clark	}	
Mr C S Marriott	}	
Extras		0
Total (15 overs) (0 wkts)		25

Fall of wickets

All Ceylon XI Bowling

	O	M	R	W
de Kretser	6	2	8	0
Brindley	15.4	3	40	5
D B Gunasekara	11	1	51	2
Jayawickreme	8	1	40	1
Joseph	5	0	24	1
C H Gunasekara	4	1	16	0
D S Jayasundera	14	3	42	0

1933/34 India and Ceylon XI v Marylebone Cricket Club
Colombo Cricket Club Ground, Colombo. February 22, 23, 24,
1934
M. C. C. won by 8 runs.

M. C. C.
First innings

A H Bakewell	b Amar Singh	4
Mr W H V Levett	c Brindley b Amar Singh	6
A Mitchell	lbw b Amar Singh	1
J Langridge	lbw b Amar Singh	13
Mr B H Valentine	b Kelaart	10
L F Townsend	c Joseph b Nayudu	56
M S Nichols	b Jayawickreme	37
H Verity	c Schokman b Kelaart	15
Mr J H Human	lbw b Amar Singh	2
E W Clark	not out	7
Mr C S Marriott	b Amar Singh	1
Extras		3
Total (76.1 overs)		155

Fall of wickets   1/4, 2/11, 3/16, 4/33, 5/40, 6/128,
                         7/132, 8/136, 9/154, 10/155

India and Ceylon XI Bowling

	O	M	R	W
Amar Singh	30.1	5	62	6
Kelaart	14	8	22	2
Nayudu	16	5	35	1
Jayawickreme	5	3	3	1
Amarnath	7	1	11	0
Brindley	4	1	19	0

India and Ceylon XI
First innings

Dilawar Hussein	b Nichols	0
W T Brindley	lbw b Verity	11
V C Schokman	hit wkt b Clark	39
C S Nayudu	c Verity b Marriott	11
L Amar Singh	c Verity b Clark	0
L Amarnath	b Marriott	16
S Wazir Ali	lbw b Marriott	0
S S Jayawickreme	not out	11
N S Joseph	c Nichols b Verity	6
E G S Kelaart	lbw b Verity	7
C H Gunasekera	st Levett b Marriott	0
Extras		3
Total (39.5 overs)		104

Fall of wickets   1/1, 2/31, 3/62, 4/62, 5/63, 6/63,
7/82, 8/89, 9/103, 10/104

M. C. C. Bowling

	O	M	R	W
Marriott	15.5	3	37	4
Clark	8	3	12	2
Nichols	4	1	14	1
Verity	12	1	38	3

M. C. C.
Second innings

A H Bakewell	c Kelaart b Amar Singh	0
Mr W H V Levett	b Nayudu	7
Mr J H Human	c Schokman b Amar Singh	0
A Mitchell	b Kelaart	26
J Langridge	c Amar Singh b Kelaart	12
Mr B H Valentine	c Schokman b Jayawickreme	9
L F Townsend	c and b Kelaart	1
M S Nichols	b Kelaart	1
H Verity	st Schokman b Kelaart	5
E W Clark	not out	7
Mr C S Marriott	b Amar Singh	3
Extras		7
Total (36.4 overs)		78

Fall of wickets   1/2, 2/2, 3/16, 4/48, 5/61, 6/61,
                         7/62, 8/68, 9/71, 10/78

India and Ceylon XI Bowling

	O	M	R	W
Amar Singh	13.4	3	23	3
Kelaart	9	1	17	5
Nayudu	4	0	13	1
Jayawickreme	5	1	11	1
Armanath	5	3	7	0

India and Ceylon XI
Second innings

W T Brindley	lbw b Marriott	5
S Wazir Ali	lbw b Verity	42
C S Nayudu	b Nichols	13
L Amarnath	b Nichols	30
S S Jayawickreme	c Valentine b Verity	7
Dilawar Hussein	lbw b Clark	4
L Amar Singh	c Levett b Clark	0
N S Joseph	c Nichols b Verity	0
E G S Kelaart	b Clark	3
V C Schokman	not out	1
C H Gunasekera	b Clarke	13
Extras		3
Total (44 overs)		121

Fall of wickets   1/13, 2/46, 3/91, 4/93, 5/103,
                       6/103, 7/103, 8/103, 9/106, 10/121

M. C. C. Bowling

	O	M	R	W
Marriott	8	2	15	1
Clark	13	3	38	4
Nichols	12	2	42	2
Verity	9	2	23	3
Langridge	2	2	0	0

Appendix II

Summary details of non-first class matches played by MCC on their tour of India in 1933/34

At Karachi, October 15, 16, 1933. C B Rubie's XI versus MCC
MCC   292 & 70 for four dec.
C B Rubie's XI   99 & 103 for six.   Match drawn

At Karachi, October 18, 19, 1933. Karachi XI versus MCC
MCC   362 for eight dec.
Karachi XI   89 & 112 for four.   Match drawn

At Peshawar, October 28, 29, 1933. North West Frontier Provinces versus MCC
NWF Provinces   94 & 121.
MCC   350 for seven dec.   MCC won by an
                                                innings and 135 runs

At Lahore, November 1, 2, 1933. Punjab Governor's XI versus MCC
MCC   402 for seven dec.
Governor's XI   253 for eight   Match drawn

At Lahore, November 4, 5, 1933. Northern India versus MCC
Northern India   53 & 58
MCC   246 for seven dec.   MCC won by an
                                                innings and 135 runs

At New Delhi, November 18, 19, 1933. Delhi and District versus MCC
Delhi and District   98 & 102
MCC   333   MCC won by an
                                                innings and 133 runs

At Jamnagar, December 3, 4, 1933. Jamnagar versus MCC
Jamnagar   90 & 45 for six
MCC   151 for eight dec.   Match drawn

At Bombay, December 12, 13, 1933. Bombay City versus MCC
Bombay City   140 & 56 for two
MCC   319 for eight dec.   Match drawn

At Poona, December 20, 21, 1933. Poona XI versus MCC
MCC   161 for five dec.
Poona XI   3 & 39 for two   Match drawn

At Calcutta, December 27, 1933. British in Bengal versus MCC
MCC   187 for five dec.
British in Bengal   121 for eight   Match drawn

At Calcutta, December 28, 1933. Indians and Anglo-Indians in Bengal
versus MCC
Indians and Anglo-Indians in Bengal   123
MCC   79 for six   MCC won by eight
                                                wickets. (England
                                                batted on.)

At Indore, January 16, 17, 1934. Central India versus MCC
MCC   157 & 52 for no wicket
Central India   157   Match drawn

At Mysore, January 28, 29, 1934. Mysore versus MCC
MCC   451 for seven dec. & 72 for no wkt dec.
Mysore   107 & 56   MCC won by 360
                                                runs

At Madras, February 7, 1934. Indian Cricket Federation XI versus MCC

MCC	268 for six dec.	
Indian Cricket Federation XI	81	MCC won by 187 runs

At Galle, February 23, 1934. Galle versus MCC

Galle	79 for seven dec.	
MCC	59 for two	Match Drawn

At Darrawella, February 26, 1934. Up-Country XI versus MCC

MCC	228 for two dec. & 53 for one dec.	
Up-Country XI	72 and 100 for two	MCC won by 156 runs on first innings

Appendix III

MCC Tour of India 1933-34
Test Match Averages

Batting

	Matches	Innings	NotOut	Runs	HS	Avge	100	50
D R Jardine	3	4	1	221	65	73.66	0	3
C F Walters	3	6	2	284	102	71.00	1	2
H Verity	3	3	1	121	55*	60.50	0	1
B H Valentine	2	3	0	179	136	59.66	1	0
H Elliott	2	2	1	51	37*	51.00	0	0
A H Bakewell	1	2	0	89	85	44.50	0	1
J Langridge	3	4	0	148	70	37.00	0	1
A Mitchell	3	5	0	114	47	22.80	0	0
L F Townsend	3	4	0	73	40	18.25	0	0
C J Barnett	3	6	1	88	33	17.60	0	0
E W Clark	3	3	1	15	10	7.50	0	0
W H V Levett	1	2	1	7	5	7.00	0	0
M S Nichols	3	4	0	24	13	6.00	0	0

Bowling

	Overs	Mdns	Runs	Wickets	BB	Avge
H Verity	157.5	61	387	23	7-49	16.82
J Langridge	90	28	192	10	5-63	19.20
M S Nichols	113.1	31	287	13	5-55	22.07
E W Clark	100.3	26	263	10	3-39	26.30
L F Townsend	43	14	132	2	2-22	66.00

MCC Tour of India 1933-34
Tour Averages – First Class Matches

Batting

	Matches	Innings	NotOut	Runs	HS	Avge	100	50
D R Jardine	14	19	3	835	102	52.18	2	5
C F Walters	11	18	2	689	102	43.06	1	6
B H Valentine	14	22	1	834	145	39.71	2	4
C J Barnett	16	25	1	880	140	36.66	3	3
L F Townsend	15	22	4	566	93*	31.44	0	4
J Langridge	14	19	3	487	70	30.43	0	2
A H Bakewell	11	18	2	479	158	29.93	1	2
A Mitchell	13	21	0	616	161	29.33	1	3
H Verity	14	18	4	384	91*	27.42	0	2
R J Gregory	10	15	2	349	148	26.84	1	1
H Elliott	7	5	1	89	37*	22.25	0	0
M S Nichols	14	22	3	400	79	21.05	0	4
J H Human	10	14	2	186	48	15.50	0	0
W H V Levett	12	18	6	144	25	12.00	0	0
E W Clark	14	14	8	62	11	10.33	0	0
C S Marriott	9	9	1	26	8	3.25	0	0

Bowling

	Overs	Mdns	Runs	Wickets	BB	Avge
L F Townsend	242.3	72	608	43	7-16	14.13
H Verity	487.2	79	1,180	78	7-37	15.12
E W Clark	381.1	111	890	56	6-24	15.89
A Mitchell	9	1	32	2	1-10	16.00
M S Nichols	344.2	70	989	55	5-14	17.98
J Langridge	262.5	97	585	31	5-63	18.87
C S Marriott	288.4	103	669	32	6-35	20.90
J H Human	51.3	5	220	7	2-21	31.42
B H Valentine	13	2	48	1	1-19	48.00
R J Gregory	16	3	51	1	1-19	51.00
C J Barnett	80	22	211	3	2-26	70.33

Also bowled: D R Jardine 2 – 0 – 6 – 0;   C F Walters   2 – 1 – 8 – 0

Select Bibliography

Bombay Chronicle

Douglas, Christopher: *Douglas Jardine: Spartan Cricketer*, London

Guha, Ramachandra: *The Indian History of British Sport*

John Wisden's Cricketers' Almanack, 1935

Illustrated Weekly of India

Lonely Planet Guide to India, London

Lonsdale Book of Cricket, London

Mais, S P B: *The Unknown Island*

Misra, Maria: *India Since the Great Rebellion*

The Independent, London

The Spectator, London

The Times, London

The Times of India

Tribune, Bombay

Index

Allen, G O B, 'Gubby' 12, 14,
   23, 31
Amarnath, Lala 42–3, 73–4,
   80, 92

Bakewell, A H 17–9, 107
Barne, Rt Rev George, Bishop
   of Lahore 50
Barnett, C J 17, 19, 34–5, 57,
   62, 86, 98
Bedser, Alec 13
'bodyline' 1, 4, 12, 17, 19
Boucheron, Louis 6
Bradman, Don 2, 12, 18,
   30–1, 119

Cartier, Jacques 5–7
Clark, E W 17, 19, 42, 57, 66,
   86, 112
Compton, Denis 12–3, 27

Duleepsinhji, K S 4, 5, 8, 31,
   34, 61, 66
Dungapur, Maharawal of 58

Dyer, General 41–2

East India Company 27
Eden Gardens 81, 85
Elliott, C H 17, 20, 73, 85

First World War 17

Gandhi, Mrs Indira 41
Gandhi, Mahatma 11, 41, 55
Golden Temple, Amritsar
   40–2
Gregory, R J 17, 20, 67, 98
Guha, Ramachandra 7, 29, 33,
   40, 50, 55, 70, 72, 80, 90

Hazare, V S 79
Hobbs, Jack 102
Holkar, Maharaja of 29, 30
Hosie, A L 56, 80–1
Human, J H 17, 20–1, 66, 92

Jam Sahib of Nawanagar,
   Maharaja of 5, 42, 61, 66

Kashmir, Maharaja of 1

Jackson, Sir Stanley 106
Jardine, D R
  and Australians 13–6
  and game shooting 60–1,
    66, 78, 93, 118
  and school cricket 14
  and Surrey CCC 1, 2, 118
  and the Viceroy 50, 52
  as journalist 2
  as MCC captain 1, 2, 12,
    28, 78
  bodyline controversy 1, 3, 4,
    5, 30–1
  Indian roots 31–2
  marriage 3
  umpiring controversy 106,
    112

Langridge, James 17, 21, 25, 107
Larwood, Harold 4, 5, 12–3,
  19, 23, 31, 33
Levett, W H V 17, 21, 25,
  34–5, 85–6, 107

Marriott, C S 17, 22, 33, 36,
  79, 80, 97, 107
Merchant, Vijay 67, 73, 113
Mitchell, A 17, 23, 25, 52, 66,
  73, 98, 107, 113
Moin-ud-Dowlah, Nawab of
  29, 35, 106

Nayudu, Major C K 19,
  28–30, 40, 47, 52, 56, 73,
    78, 80–1, 92–3, 97–8,
    106, 112, 119
Nichols, M S 17–8, 23, 52, 56,
  80
Nissar, M 86, 92

Pakistan 8, 26, 29, 33, 47
Pataudi, Nawab of 4, 5, 12,
  30–1
Patiala, Maharaja of 5–7, 42–3,
  47, 50, 52, 112
'Patiala peg' 42–3
Patiala, Yuvraj of 42–3, 50,
  112
Porbandar, Maharaja of 1, 5, 6

Ranjitsinhji, K S 5, 6, 8, 31,
  42, 51, 61, 66
Rubie, C B 34

Sebastien, Lalla 32, 70, 72
Second World War 17–8, 23
Sutcliffe, Herbert 13, 102

Tarrant, Frank 47, 73, 86, 92,
  101, 106, 112
Townsend, L F 17–8, 23–4,
  34, 57–8, 61, 81

Underwood, Derek 18, 20

Valentine, B H 17, 24–5, 34,
  51–2, 61, 73, 86, 107
Verity, Hedley 17–9, 21, 25,
  31, 35, 52, 62, 66, 79, 81,
    107, 113

Vizianagram, Maharaja Kumar
    of 5, 6, 29, 92, 113
Voce, Bill 12, 23, 31
Walters, C F 17–8, 24–5, 34,
    52, 58, 66, 73, 79, 105,
    107

Warner, Sir Pelham 13, 14
Wazir Ali, S 47, 52, 56, 92
Willingdon, Earl of 7, 29, 30,
    32, 40–1, 52, 55–6, 90,
    119
  Lady 30, 50